S0-DVE-740

# Good Divorces, Bad Divorces

## *A Case for Divorce Mediation*

**Joyce Hauser**

University Press of America, Inc.
Lanham • New York • London

Copyright © 1995 by
University Press of America,® Inc.
4720 Boston Way
Lanham, Maryland 20706

3 Henrietta Street
London, WC2E 8LU England

All rights reserved
Printed in the United States of America
British Cataloging in Publication Information Available

ISBN 0-8191-9856-0 (pbk: alk ppr)

⊖™ The paper used in this publication meets the minimum
requirements of American National Standard for Information
Sciences—Permanence of Paper for Printed Library Materials,
ANSI Z39.48—1984

To Ellen, not only my daughter and friend, but someone, who helped as editor, proofreader, and sounding board, and to my sons Mark and Mitchell, all of whom have enriched my life.

# Contents

# PREFACE

In doing the research for this book, I learned that Americans do not handle confrontation well, especially when it comes to the greatest conflict in their personal lives - the break-up of a marriage. While examining the material from hundreds of individuals, who responded to my questionnaire, written or scrawled in a heavy hand, or underlined more than once with rows of exclamation points afterward, it became apparent that, many of these divorced men and women were, for the most part, extremely angry. Whether it had been a year since the decree or more than a decade, they still held that ax in their hands. They hated the divorce. They hated the ex-spouse. In many cases, they hated the lawyer(s).

Any cry for human change, such as divorce, has meant some involvement in our legal system and the stigma of being called before a judge. Terms such as adversarial lawyers and protracted litigation become part of two innocent people's lives who have not broken any laws. And unless there is real abuse, I believe that two people should not be treated as criminals in a court system which is over-crowded and understaffed.

The adversarial legal system, through which divorce and

custody fights are supposedly settled, attempts to apply a legal solution to what is essentially a highly charged, emotional problem. When the decision to end a marriage is made, a person is rarely placed in a more stressful situation - emotionally, financially and legally.

Ideally, mediation is best for advancing harmony and justice in our lives. However, according to my study, if given the choice, most people will not choose mediation to resolve conflicts but will choose to fight, or, better yet, look to the legal system to fight for them. They question how two people, who are ending a marriage and fraught with anger and hostilities, are expected to sit together and peacefully work out the dissolution of their partnership.

My premise for this exploratory study is that public relations can help our complex, pluralistic society to reach decisions and to function more effectively by contributing to mutual understanding about divorce mediation among groups and institutions. It serves to bring the public and public policies into accord by disseminating the information in order to help divorcing people make better decisions.

Concurrently, the field of mediation needs to understand the attitudes and values of their public in order to apply the proper strategies to bring about social change. Clearly, this analysis of a target audience's discourse identifies issues which pave the way for the public relations effort.

In practice, public relations consists of a coordinated program of research, analysis and communication. The goal is to create, build and maintain mutually beneficial exchange relationships in order to satisfy human needs and wants.

Gathering a complete collection of all that is known about the situation, forces operating on it, and those involved or affected, internally and externally, I fused my twenty years of social psychology and public relations experience with my study of mediation in order to define roles, the mission and prepare action plans.

The pages, which follow, will deal rarely with

philosophy, psychology, or how to mediate, but will concentrate instead on strategies for influencing consumer behavior, communications, and the efficient use of mass media aimed at special populations. Attitude, behavior, images, credibility, and demographics are, after all, the language of public relations. Perhaps, they express the spirit as well.

# INTRODUCTION

What is mediation?

Mediation is a form of conflict resolution, in which two or more people, who have a dispute, voluntarily agree to meet with an impartial third party in order to find a mutually acceptable way of settling their dispute.

What is a mediator?

A mediator is a person who acts as an impartial third party in a dispute. Mediators are not judges. Instead, their role is to assist people involved in a dispute to find a resolution by using structured, productive communication, and problem-solving techniques. A mediator does not take sides; the mediator does not decide who is right or wrong; nor does the mediator force parties into an agreement. The mediator does not set the terms of the agreement, but facilitates a decision of terms which the parties find mutually acceptable.

## Why mediation?

The job of the mediator is to identify and help resolve the underlying cause of the dispute. Unlike the courts' sole job of determining who is guilty and who is not, the mediator must help the parties talk it out unrestrained by questions of admissibility. The mediator should be able to help the parties concentrate on what should be done in the future, rather than on punishment and revenge, or "who is responsible" for "what event," which may have occurred in the past. The parties' perceptions of what the other has said or done may be distorted. As the mediator listens to each of them, he/she provides a sounding board for the parties' thoughts and feelings, while looking for the underlying causes of the conflict and possible solutions, the mediator can begin to open channels of communication and take the first steps towards a long-lasting resolution.

## How to start mediating?

When two parties start out in mediation they usually are quite angry with each other. Although they agree to go, most of the time they feel they are in the wrong place and question what they have walked into. A mediator has to calm the anger and build trust.

The first thing the mediator does is explain his/her role and that he/she is not there as a partisan or spokesperson for either side. Once one party feels the mediator is leaning too much toward the other's favor the credibility and ability to function as an intermediary comes to an end.

After the mediator has explained to the parties what the process and the role of the mediator is, the parties can clarify their motivations for seeking mediation. At this beginning stage, one or both parties are so nervous they will agree to anything without understanding the process. Therefore, it is important, in addition to explaining the process, that the mediator sets the tone, to create informality, directness, receptivity, and to work toward establishing contact between the mediator and the parties and between the parties themselves.

The techniques of mediation:

Mediation is much harder than just giving advice or making decisions which are to be accepted. Reflect on your own experience and you will know that this is so. People do not like to be told what to do. They also will not make a decision if they can avoid it. Therefore, a mediator must seek the acceptable solution and press for it without overstepping and imposing it, without letting his/her own judgments and values intrude. This is difficult. It requires patience, sensitivity and clear thinking.

Gathering information:

The goal of the mediator and parties is to set out all necessary information to identify the particular issues needing resolution and the dimensions of those issues. This involves identifying all relevant facts, including economic, emotional, or other factors involved in each party's view of any particular issue.

At this informational stage, it is important that the mediator allow the parties room to explain the significance of any particular issue. The mediator continually focuses on what the parties describe as the content of the issues, and how the parties talk about these issues. In this respect, the mediator will notice patterns between the parties, such as one party blaming the other, or accommodating the wishes of the other.

Resolving conflict:

The major work for the mediator is to help the parties move past unproductive patterns of conflict, which exist between them, and to work toward collaborative and productive ways of exploring the issues. The most essential aspect of this process is the identification by each party of their respective needs, underlying specific and concrete issues, and moving toward resolution based on a mutual sense of fairness.

The mediator gives feedback to the parties on the agreements such as whether the agreement is realistic. However, the mediator's view is never asserted. The mediator asks questions in order to determine whether they have fully understood the implications of particular issues.

Reaching agreement:

Once a concrete agreement has been reached, the mediator's task is to draft the agreement. It is important to use words which are both understandable to the parties, and which reflect, as accurately as possible, their intentions as to what the agreement is, and how it will take effect.

# CHAPTER 1

## A Survey of Divorced Parents and Their Attitudes Toward Ex-Spouses, Litigation, and Mediation

In order to create an extensive and positive recognition of divorce mediation as a profession and to stimulate harmony and good will between the providers and components of the system at each and every point of contact, one must first look at the American men and women who separate and divorce.

Who are the divorced Americans? How do they behave in the face of divorce? How do they make their decisions on choosing an attorney or other professionals with whom they will work? Perhaps just as important, in retrospect, how do they view the experience of divorce in terms of its psychological, emotional and financial reverberations?

In order to begin to explore some of these issues, a survey of divorced men and women living in the tri-state area of New York, New Jersey, and Pennsylvania was conducted. On

April 25, 1988, a 21-item questionnaire was mailed to the 2,750 members of Kindred Spirits, an organization of single parents with children. (See Appendix)

A cover letter explained the purpose of the survey: "to assess how men and women view the strengths and the weaknesses of the court system's handling of separation and divorce." The survey was conducted under the auspices of the American Arbitration Association, and their pamphlet "Family Mediation Rules" was enclosed in the letters sent in order to acquaint members with the mediation process. All responses were anonymous.

A total of 392 questionnaires were returned - a response rate of more than 14.25 percent. Of the respondents, 181 were men and 211 were women.

Members of an organization such as Kindred Spirits are self-selected, and many possess certain social or psychological characteristics which led to their interest in or need for such an association.

This sample, which proved to be an educated and affluent group, may represent just the sort of consumer that mediators and mediation services hope to target. Their responses are valuable, as insight into the attitudes of a specific sub-group of divorced men and women, and as general guidelines for marketing research.

By approaching the phenomenon of divorce mediation as it exists in the 1990s - in terms of its history, complexities, methodologies, advantages, and prospects for the future, along with the Kindred Spirits survey and other recent research - a multifaceted picture of potential, public relations challenges emerges.

The seven categories, which follow, have been simplified for ease of discussion. In some cases, they also have been translated into fictional consumer quotes with the same goal in mind. The everyday language of both the consumer and the marketer helps us focus on the real attitudes with which we are faced.

## Awareness

The unfortunate truth is that the vast majority of American men and women have never heard of divorce mediation. Or, if they have heard of the term, they have defined it subconsciously as "nothing new" and have given little or no further thought to the concept.

This is, at first, both discouraging and somewhat difficult to believe. The books written on the subject in the past decade could fill an entire shelf in a city bookstore. Dozens of articles have explained and/or praised divorce mediation on the pages of major women's magazines, general interest magazines and some of the nation's largest-circulation, daily newspapers. In a media- and information-saturated culture, however, this is simply not enough.

Perhaps the best-known professions in the world are those played by actors in motion pictures and on television. Doctors, lawyers, police officers, private detectives and prostitutes are among the most frequently seen working people on the screen. These portrayals affect our opinions, interest and perceptions of people and work (Slaby and Quarforth 1980).

In fact, there are far more law-related jobs in television's version of the work world than in the actual labor force (Jeffries-Fox and Signorielli 1982). Research shows that, when young viewers are asked to estimate the percentage of the population involved in law enforcement, the estimates are far higher than reality, but consistent with what is shown on television (Abel, Fontes, Greendberg, and Atkin 1981).

It is clear that screen portrayals affect real-life occupational choices as well. The year after the release of "All the President's Men," enrollment in journalism schools soared (Gates 1982).

Media's impact on the public can change perceptions and attitudes toward a profession. Perhaps if the NBC-TV series, "L.A. Law," had premiered in 1986 as "L.A. Mediator," a far greater number of divorcing couples would be seeking mediation already. But the continuing saga of two peaceful and reasonable people coming to a civilized divorce agreement may not be the makings of high drama.

The bottom line, as illustrated by the Kindred Spirits survey, is that the majority of married, separated and divorced couples in the United States have not heard of divorce mediation, and would not know where to find a mediator, should they need one. It is unlikely that they will find a mediator as a result of shopping for the best possible professional to represent them in a divorce since the survey indicates that most divorcing men and women do very little research on the people they hire.

The American public still thinks of divorce almost exclusively in adversarial terms. Again, this is partially a result of the messages about divorce, which come to us from the news and entertainment media.

## Confusion

"If you don't believe mediation would have worked for you," the survey asked, "why not?"

A number of respondents gave answers that indicated a complete lack of understanding of the term - Mediation. An engineer explained that it was because he "wanted out of the relationship." A business owner said he and his ex-wife could not have used mediation because they are "both happier alone." Others answered the question by citing reasons the marriage had been a mistake.

What is the source of this confusion? There may be several, including the mere sound of the word. The interdisciplinary nature of divorce mediation, admirable in many ways, may be highly confusing to the public such as:

  - Divorce mediation is something lawyers do, and the American Bar Association has drawn up guidelines for its practice. But divorce mediation is also something social workers and psychological counselors do.

- Divorce mediation is not therapy.  But a lot of therapists say they do mediation.
- Divorce mediation is something that mental health professionals do on the side, in addition to their regular practice or as part of couples counseling.  But its most vocal advocates insist that it is a separate profession; one which requires special training and skills.

The debate goes on.  And although there are those who insist that the arguments are unnecessary - that mediation can be all these things and more - even this attitude does little to solve the problem.  In fact, it may complicate things further.  If current books on the subject describe three different overall models of divorce mediation, how can the process be described to the public in fast, potent, easy-to-understand language?

Mediation, purely defined as a process, is not a tremendously complex concept.  However, the divorce mediator must keep in mind the nature and attitude of his or her audience.


## Negative Views of Divorce

In the late 1960s and early 1970s, peace and love were the watchwords of much of the Baby Boom generation.  No higher compliment could be paid, it seemed, than to describe someone as a warm and loving human being.  A famous "Life" magazine photograph of 1967 showed a young student with blond hair falling into his eyes, who calmly placed a carnation in the rifle barrels of army guards on the Pentagon steps.

In 1967 mediation - had it been well-established - might have been the only socially acceptable way to end a marriage.  The ideal ex-spouses would still hug and smile beatifically when they met.  Today, the emotional attitudes that mediation evokes are out of fashion.  If the essential purpose of mediation throughout the world and throughout the centuries has been the restoration of natural harmony, it is a measure out of step with the 1990s.

The divorcing public seems singularly unimpressed even with the most practical advantage of divorce mediation - its low cost. The majority does not take cost into consideration, when choosing an attorney, even though they may complain loudly about the bill afterward. Many prospective consumers seem to take the attitude that "you get what you pay for." A number of participants in the Kindred Spirits survey, who had an adversarial divorce and felt they "lost," blamed themselves for having spent too little, and, therefore, deserved the unhappy outcome.

If divorce mediation can result in a less expensive divorce, some ask, how can it possibly be the best alternative?

The Kindred Spirits survey turned up a number of divorced men and women who had tried mediation and had been unhappy with the practitioner, the results, or both. A negative correlation did appear - those who had tried divorce mediation in the past were less likely to recommend it to friends in the future than people unfamiliar with the concept.

Elsewhere (Kelly 1989), results were more positive. The mediation respondents were significantly more satisfied with almost every aspect of the mediation process and the outcome compared to the adversarial couples.


## They Want an Advocate All Their Own


If attorneys are so unpopular, and research indicates some strong negative attitudes toward the legal profession, then why does everybody want one so badly?

Lawyers are there, at least in theory, to protect the client's interest. In the Kindred Spirits survey, women were especially likely to mention the importance of having a good representative, someone officially and completely in one's corner. If this conjures up an image of two boxers waiting for the bell to signal the start of the first round, it is neither accidental nor inappropriate.

Many divorcing men and women do see the divorce case as a boxing match of sorts. The high-priced divorce lawyer is the trainer and manager, the expert with all the answers and all the experience, advising the fighter on strategy and technique. Fortunately or unfortunately, they see the divorce mediator (if they see him or her at all) as the referee, the impartial person who steps in only when the rules are being broken.

Even this analogy falls short, however, of describing the true expectations of the husband or wife who retains an attorney. Many want a great deal more than advice and expertise; they hope for a surrogate, someone who will step into the ring in the client's place and fight the battles against the spouse-opponent. The idealized attorney never gives into the spouse-opponent's demands, never tires of fighting, and never gives up until the spouse-client is victorious. Once such an attorney is found, the spouse-client dreams that he or she can relax, sit back and simply gloat over the wins to come. It is perhaps the emotional equivalent of running home in tears, then having Daddy, Big Brother or some other large strong defender go back and show that bully who's boss.

Understandably, at least one spouse in a divorce case may well be feeling victimized by the other; at times, both spouses see themselves in that role. Comments like "I just can't win," "he/she just won't talk," or he/she just won't listen" are common.

Rather than coming in with the strength, safety and security of a defender, divorce mediation demands that both spouses behave like grown-ups, even if they feel victimized. The quieter or less aggressive of the two may reject the idea of mediation in the very beginning, convinced that he or she will have to fight for opportunities to speak and/or endure the same sort of verbal bullying experienced during the marriage.

The lawyer and the legal system are seen as protection. Despite the high rate of non-compliance with child support payment and other divorce-related mandates, most Americans still have faith in the power of the judge to move mountains. After all, his or her word is literally law.

There also appears to be a strong, almost unshakable belief in the inevitability of pure and true justice. We all like to believe that few murderers go free, and that few innocent people are punished for crimes they did not commit. It should be apparent, however, that in cases where right and wrong are less clearly defined, the scales of justice may not always be perfectly balanced.

Among Kindred Spirits survey participants, who believed that the attorneys involved had an effect on the outcome of the divorce case, the prevailing opinion was that the other spouse's attorney had been superior, and, therefore, the terms were not what the survey participant had wanted. Rarely do divorcing men and women, who see themselves as having "won" in a divorce, think it is because their lawyers were better. They believe they have won because they were in the right.

### They Believe It Won't Work

For many prospective users of divorce mediation, the desire for an advocate goes further than a mere belief that one is in better hands with an attorney than with some other kind of professional. There is a strongly held belief that because mediation is unconnected to the legal system, it simply won't work.

Divorce mediation agreements are not legally binding, opponents point out, and can give none of the protection that the court system is believed to offer. Based on the Kindred Spirits survey, more women than men appear to feel this way. One possibility is that women feel a greater need for protection from a paternalistic justice system. Another is that women are more likely to be promised payment, alimony, and/or child support in theoretically enforceable court rulings, and, therefore, have more to lose from an ex-spouse's failure to live up to such agreements.

Couples, who reject the idea of mediation, also state the belief that the process cannot work in many cases in which complex legal or financial issues are involved. Mediators, who have not attended law school, they note, don't know the ins, outs and technicalities of the laws that affect divorce. The couple and mediator could spend weeks drawing up a carefully thought out agreement, only to be told by the consulting attorney that some of its points are impossible or unacceptable from a legal point of view.

The skepticism about divorce mediation, however, goes beyond the mediator/attorney comparison. Many divorcing men and women believe that mediation cannot work because of the attitude of their spouses. Soon-to-be ex-husbands and ex-wives are described in their statements as irrational, unreasonable, angry, vengeful and/or vindictive. How, they ask, can mediation magically transform such attitudes? Even more to the point, how can the self-proclaimed reasonable spouse get the unreasonable one ever to attend an initial mediation session?

## Problems with Interprofessional Referrals and Attitudes

Why don't attorneys, psychiatrists, psychologists, therapists and social workers refer their clients and patients to divorce mediators more often?

The problem might be summed up in two sentences: Mental health professionals believe they can do the job just as well. Lawyers believe they can do it better.

Certainly, the problem is unlikely to be that simple, or that intractable. But the facts about referral are discouraging. Over half of the cases of an average, private mediator are self-referrals. And, there are simply not enough of them. The Kindred Spirits survey revealed a low rate of referrals from professionals in general. Therapists refer more patients to mediation than other professionals, and counselors refer a few. The clergy are practically making no referrals to mediation at all.

Attorneys appear to be of little help in making referrals. Divorced men and women report that among the few lawyers, who did mention mediation to their clients, most did so only to describe it as useless and/or discourage them from entering into the process. It has been suggested that the legal community considers mediation a threat in terms of competition for clients. Whether the competitive charge is true or not, lawyers as a group do tend to be more anti-mediation than in favor of it.

If there is any question about the importance of professional referrals in the growth and success of mediation, a comparison of private and public mediators makes the situation clear. Public mediators, who are affiliated with courts, receive virtually all their cases through court referrals. As a result, their caseloads are relatively high. Private mediators, on the other hand, have no such formal referral system, and all too little in the way of informal referrals. As a group, few make a living solely from practicing mediation alone.

## Issues of Credibility, Skills and Training

If twenty practicing, private divorce mediators gathered for something of a class picture, they would represent an interesting mix of trainings and backgrounds. Of the twenty, eight would be social workers, four and a half would be psychiatrists, three would be lawyers, two would be psychologists and the remaining two and a half would come from different, various backgrounds. It is no wonder that the general public has some confusion about exactly who divorce mediators are, or should be.

The lack of credibility that divorce mediation suffers from is partly a function of the practitioners' perceived lack of training. It is not due to the misconception that divorce mediators are uneducated. They are, in fact, a highly educated group with a variety of graduate degrees. Unfortunately, most Americans regard graduate degrees in Psychology or Social Work as less of an accomplishment than a law degree. And even if one does revere a graduate degree in Psychology, it is very easy for a potential client to wonder what makes a divorce mediator qualified, if there is no specific degree. The potential client could stress that the lawyer has a degree in what he or she claims to practice.

There has been a move by the Academy of Family Mediators to set up requirements for membership. But as it stands, there is neither a license nor a particular certificate required for the practice of divorce mediation. Untrained men and women are unimpeded from calling themselves mediators and establishing private or group practices.

Reprinted with the permission of Jossey-Bass Inc.

Hauser, Joyce. "An Analysis and Feasibility Study of Divorce Mediation and a Program for Its Marketing." In P.R. Maida (ed.), Mediation Quarterly, Vol. 11, No. 2, Winter 1993. Copyright 1993 by Jossey-Bass Inc., Publishers.

# CHAPTER 2

## Opportunities in Changing Human Behavior

Despite all the problems, there are positive sides to the future of divorce mediation. The greatest opportunities fall into seven overall categories.

### People Wish Their Lawyers Were More Like Mediators

Very few of the men and women, who share this wish, would see it in these terms. Most are unfamiliar with the mediation process and profession, and, therefore, they never realize that the portrait of an ideal divorce lawyer is almost an exact job description of a divorce mediator. The things that the Kindred Spirits study participants professed to miss most in their attorneys were what mediation and its practitioners offer.

Based on the Kindred Spirits survey, divorced men and women wanted their attorneys to be empathetic negotiators. While people see legal professionals as experts in negotiation, they don't view empathy as one of their strong suits, or even one of their priorities.    A professional, who combines the two qualities, would theoretically have a long line of divorcing clients waiting outside his or her office door.

Survey respondents also see accessibility as a real problem in working with attorneys.  Once the lawyer is retained, he or she is simply not available for the client's phone calls or other attempts at contact.  The impression often given to the client is that the lawyer they've chosen is just too busy for them.

Accessibility appears to be little or no problem in working with a divorce mediator.  The actual workings of the case take place in scheduled, timed sessions during which the mediator is always present.

For these reasons, the divorcing client may want to look for a lawyer who is functioning as a mediator.  Perhaps from there, any qualified mediator will be acceptable to those who seek these qualities and/or arrangements.

## Public Opinion: Lawyers and the Court Are Bad Guys

The same high visibility, media attention, and centuries of experience, which have made the legal profession so well-known to the general public, have also done damage.  Many of the divorced are antagonized and disillusioned by lawyers.  Their feelings appear to be strong, negative, and widely-held.  They are, in fact, even shared by some divorced men and women who are themselves attorneys.

Of past divorce clients, who would not recommend their lawyers, a significant number were those who had felt pressured into accepting an agreement.  The fact that the mediation process never forces spouses into an agreement can be a marketing asset.

Litigation does not make for friendly divorces.  More than half of the participants in the Kindred Spirits survey said that the legal process had hurt their relationship with their ex-spouse.  Men responded in this way more than women.  The fact that divorce mediation actually can improve the relationship of two divorcing spouses can be stressed in marketing efforts.

Beyond their feelings about and reactions to the attorneys, divorcing couples have stated strong negative reactions about the experience of going into court. At best, the court system is merely impersonal, using dry and technical language to delve into intensely emotional issues. At worst, the experience can leave respectable citizens feeling like criminals for being there. Divorce Mediation is private and personal.

## Courts are the Wrong Place for Divorce

The fact that divorces are granted in the same setting as trials held for homicides, thefts, and tax evasions should be considered a gross anachronism. A man and woman, who have decided to end their marriage, should not stand accused of having broken the law, at least not by 20th century American standards.

Perhaps divorce belonged in the 19th century American courtroom, when religious and social standards demanded that a couple's marriage vows be taken literally. In that era, a divorce was granted only under extreme circumstances and reputations of both parties suffered greatly as a result.

In the past, people took their divorces to court because there was no other choice. Some grievous wrong had to have been committed in order to justify severing the sacred bonds of marriage. The prospect of spending a lifetime with the offending spouse had to be even more horrible than the shame of life as a divorced man or woman.

This is hardly the case in the 1990s. Divorce has almost total, social acceptance today - even former presidents of the United States have ex-wives. And now that no-fault divorce is a reality throughout the country, the last logical connection between everyday divorce and the courtroom should be broken. Thus, the state of divorce could be described by century: 19th century, the era of courtroom divorce; 20th century, the era of transition; and the 21st century, the time of mediated divorce.

Most divorces do not belong in the courtroom for an additional reason - they are not simple cases of right or wrong. What is just in a divorce settlement has more to do with the individual involved than with clear cut law book issues. Perhaps, the most important evidence against litigated divorce is that it just doesn't work well for human relations. A full ten years after their divorces, many men and women were still furious at their ex-spouses.

## There Are Good Opportunities for Referral

With a few exceptions, the busiest practitioners are the public mediators who receive referrals from the court. The less busy practitioners are the private mediators, who must rely on other professionals for referrals. The good news in this situation is that the system is set up to make referrals both easy and desirable. According to the Kindred Spirits survey, more than three out of four divorces, one or both spouses seek counseling or therapy before going through with the legalities. The hours spent in a counselor's or therapist's office represent a golden opportunity to spread the message of divorce mediation. This is a good group to target for any effective, outreach program on mediation.

Research shows that marriage and family counselors make most of the professional referrals. Furthermore, they are likely to feel that divorce mediation should be left to those who are more skilled in the profession. Closer ties to this conglomerate group can be made through their professional associations and through their conferences.

## People Believe They Should Think Highly of the Profession

Although this decade has not been characterized by a higher sense of personal morality in business, the majority of Americans still state a belief in strict ethical behavior within family and romantic relationships. They know that they should look favorably on the mediation process, whether they have used it or not.

Mediation is a fair, peaceful, honest, and upright process. Anyone, who argues against its intentions, sets himself or herself up for criticism. One might as well voice disapproval of motherhood, the American flag, or apple pie.

Participants in the Kindred Spirits survey felt that they should at least try to talk civilly with their spouse about differences on custody and settlement. Two out of three wrote that they do believe divorce mediation can help in theory. And many said they would recommend divorce mediation to friends, even if they felt it would not benefit them personally. Any educational, outreach program must take this attitude into account.

Since people do believe that mediation is a good thing to do for the children, this belief should be emphasized since children are the innocent by-standers who suffer the greatest amount from divorce. Mediators must point out that a mediated divorce is far less likely to upset or even traumatize children than a bitterly-fought custody battle in court.

## Mediators Are Highly Educated People

Eight out of every ten divorce mediators practicing today have graduate or professional degrees. This high educational level should be stressed in outreach programs. A higher awareness of these academic credentials can be helpful in countering the public perception that divorce lawyers know a great deal more than divorce mediators.

## Mediation Has Real Benefits

If the better product or better person always won, the business of Public Relations might never have become so important. Divorce mediation's inherent superiority in so many ways is not enough to guarantee its acceptance, but its numerous benefits, both real and perceived, must be conveyed to its prospective users.

Research has shown that the following benefits are inclusive in the advantages of divorce mediation.

- Keeps all divorce discussion more focused than client-attorney meetings in litigated divorce.
- Gives both spouses an opportunity to express their individual points of view.
- Saves time and money.
- Keeps the participants out of court.  Spouses who enter mediation are less likely to end up going into a court trial.
- Allows both spouses to keep control over their future circumstances instead of handing it over to lawyers.
- Balances communication between the spouses, especially helpful if one spouse in the past has not always had equal time in arguments and discussions.
- Can raise self-esteem since both spouses feel competent for having successfully managed mediation.
- Leaves the non-custodial parent (most often the father) happier with visitation and other custody-related arrangements.
- Results in fewer visitation infractions than litigated divorce.
- It works.  Three out of four couples who start mediation go on with it, and the minority reach mutually satisfactory agreements.

## <u>Conclusion</u>

The day when the study of conflict resolution is accepted universally will be the day when divorce mediation outreach programs will no longer be necessary. It will be a known alternative, accepted or rejected based on pertinent information and its helpful qualities for the person.

Until this time educational outreach programs for related professionals, media, and prospective clients must be relied upon to increase the presence and importance of the profession.

# CHAPTER 3

## Principles of Behavior

Our primary concern always must be the subjective world of the individual. In this private consciousness, what motivates him or her to choose a certain product or service? What motivates that same person to reject another product or service, especially when objective data show it to be equal or superior in quality to the one actually purchased? How does he or she feel about certain products or services, after having bought and/or used them?

These decisions are made in a highly complex mental and physical environment. Therefore, the study of consumer behavior becomes the study of many sciences: economics (including the basic concept of supply and demand), psychology (cues and symbols), social psychology (the social rewards, perceptions and sanctions that accompany certain purchases and ownerships), economic psychology (psychology of saving and spending money), sociology (particularly role theory and the role expectations of those around us) and even anthropology (the cultural myths, folklore and past, behavioral patterns that may influence behavior today).

Earlier in this century, copywriter J. Sterling Gechtel observed that people buy for emotional reasons, and then explain their purchases with rational ones (Runyon and Stewart 1987). The divorce mediator will do well to keep this wisdom in mind and present his or her service in ways that will be persuasive on both levels.


## Social Change


How do we begin to change attitudes and behavior in the population that we are most interested in?

First America must be persuaded to think about the concept of divorce mediation itself. Presently, America doesn't understand it. Most people have never heard of it.

Thanks to the centuries-old and widespread awareness of the legal profession, people assume that there is only one way to go about getting a divorce. Once a person has announced his or her intention of leaving, a call to the lawyer is made. It is, in fact, a cliche found in films, novels and, perhaps, in real life.

It is seven in the evening. The husband, Frank Smith, enters his suburban living room for what he believes will be just another quiet evening at home. But the children are nowhere to be found, and his wife explains that they've been sent to the neighbors or to her mother's for a few hours. She begins quietly to explain that she knows about the affair, or that she is involved with someone herself, or that she has given their marriage a great deal of thought, and she isn't getting what she wants and needs from their marriage.

The husband looks puzzled, annoyed, or a combination of both. Why is she bringing this up tonight, when he has so much on his mind already? Is this going to be another one of those heart-to-heart talks in which he always feels like the villain? How will he get out of this one, and why should he be put in this position time after time?

"Can't we talk about this some other night, Felicia?" He sighs. "I just spent three hours trying to convince a $5 million client not to switch agencies, and frankly all I want to deal with right now is a gin and tonic, something to eat and eight hours of uninterrupted sleep."

"You don't understand," she answers. And then she speaks the words which change everything: "I've seen a lawyer." (This scenario might as easily have been drawn using a man as an example. Whether his was a traditional union or a more contemporary two-paycheck, two career marriage, he is likely to have equally strong, if not identical reactions.)

For the advocates of divorce mediation, it may be too late to reach Felicia. She has made the traditional move that will lead to the dissolution of their marriage. The ultimate acceptance of divorce mediation lies in reaching her and her husband long before they take on the roles of the divorcing couple. From a public relations point of view, what Felicia has done already and what Frank is thinking in the middle of this scene are crucial issues.

It is likely that Frank's head is spinning. He hadn't expected this, but he knows that he has to make some response. He may argue to convince her that this move is wrong. If he is unsuccessful, however, he eventually must announce some kind of action himself. Assuming that divorce mediation has yet to make its mark on the consciousness of adult America, he will find his own lawyer. And yet, another case of adversarial, litigated divorce will be underway.

Perhaps, if this scene takes place in the year 1999, it will be played differently in many homes. Perhaps Felicia will drop her bomb by saying, "I've asked Larry (their mutual attorney) to recommend a divorce mediator." Or perhaps Frank will respond to her original announcement of having been in touch with a lawyer by saying: "There's no need for that. I won't be unreasonable. Let's behave like civilized adults, and find a mediator to work out the agreement."

Abraham Maslow (1970) developed the model of Hierarchy of Needs to explain modern-day motivations. Human needs are placed on a pyramid: those on the bottom must be satisfied before a human being can give thought to the set of needs above them. From the bottom up, Maslow explained our needs as follows:

**Physical needs**: food, water, sleep, sex.
**Safety and security needs**: stability, order, predictability, freedom from fear, harm or injury.
**Social needs**: being a part of a social group, including acceptance, approval, affection.
**Esteem needs**: competence, confidence, recognition from others.
**Self-actualization needs**: self-fulfillment, living up to one's potential.

For divorce mediation, Maslow's model presents some disturbing gaps.

The American woman embarking on the divorce process is likely to have most of her basic physical needs met. If she has been supported financially by her husband in the past, she may have some concern about future bills, and she may lose some sleep. Certainly, her sex life may change or become non-existent. But, in general, her most crucial physical needs are being met. She has enough food, water and sleep to ensure that there is no threat to her survival.

The second level of the pyramid, however, is a completely different story. The stability and order of her entire world is likely to be upset by the prospect of divorce. Either she or her husband is likely to have moved out of the family home recently, or to be on the verge of that move. A daily existence, which may have held all too much predictability, suddenly offers little of such reassuring patterns.

Fear is a very real emotion for her. She may be afraid of the changes ahead - how she will raise her children?, whether she will ever find love again?, how she will support herself?, and any number of other possibilities. Her former ally, her husband, is the enemy. She even may be specifically afraid of the sort of charges and demands he is going to make as part of the divorce process.

A friend may urge her not to be depressed - to realize that she is a terrific woman with a wonderful career. However the woman may feel more likely that her whole life has been turned upside down. She may begin to think that being successful does not matter, if you have no one to share it with. By having such feelings, she is agreeing with Maslow's Hierarchy of Needs.

Standing shakily on Level One of Maslow's pyramid and Level Two crumbling like falling bricks about her, she grasps for any support. And most often than not she finds safety with the divorce lawyer, thereby regrouting some bricks of Level Two back together. It looks like a good choice at the time. As the Kindred Spirits study indicates, divorced people hold a high regard for the protection provided by the legal profession and the court system. Whether this hypothetical woman will truly find safety and security by turning the situation over to a high-powered lawyer becomes irrelevant to her. She believes that it will, and that allows her to relax on this particular level. The end result of divorce mediation would be superior to that of litigation; however, our hypothetical woman is unable to see that far.

Divorce mediation ignores Level Two and even Level Three, and focuses on the top of the pyramid. Advocates of mediation will tell the frightened prospective consumer to consider his/her self-esteem (Level Four). Entering and successfully completing mediation helps the client feel like a more competent and confident human being. The advocate will continue to ask the client to think about how the experience will be fulfilling (Level Five). After all, the ex-spouse will be the parent of the children forever; and mediation will lead to the best human relationship amongst them all.

These are reasonable words seen from an objective point of view. However, the woman or man in the basement during an earthquake (Level One) will not hear them.

## Physical Surroundings

If a bracelet with clear-colored stones and a yellow-metal setting is displayed in a shopping-center, discount store, most consumers will assume that it is an inexpensive costume jewelry set, at best, in gold plate. The same bracelet, displayed in a jewelry case at Tiffany or Cartier, would be perceived very differently.

With jewelry, of course, there are scientific tests to determine what is genuine and what is fake, what is high quality and what is not. With many products and services, however, quality is very much a matter of perception. This is why the physical surroundings in which products and services are displayed and sold is a crucial issue.

This is especially true for a specific social class or lifestyle group. The overall atmosphere must suggest that this is for "people like us" because the consumer may well want to enjoy the product's or service's class qualities. The physical surroundings become part of the consumption process.

Ideally, physical surroundings will make a congruent statement appealing to all senses: sight, sound, touch, smell, and taste. In the case of divorce mediation, the interior design of a mediator's office must make this statement. Keeping in mind the need to portray mediation as both the civilized way to handle divorce and the route to a truly successful divorce, it is understandable that the ideal mediator's office should be symbolic of both civility and success. Individual mediators and mediation services can, of course, make personal decisions about the physical surroundings of their own offices.

When a mediator's office is represented in a television commercial message, in a television interview, or in a still photograph accompanying a press kit, it should evoke these qualities. In media images, it is recommended that the mediator's office be decorated with traditional, library-like furniture. At least one wall should be lined with bookshelves to symbolize knowledge and formal education. Diplomas and certificates on walls can also add to that impression. The mediator's desk should be a large and traditional one in a dark wood, with high-quality desk accessories, perhaps of leather and brass. Lighting should appear to be reasonably low, and the mood should be one of calm and quiet. The Asian influence on mediation might be suggested by a piece or two of Asian art in the office, or by prominently displaying textbooks on the Japanese history of mediation, or by both.

Just as the appearance and demeanor of a receptionist becomes a part of an office surrounding, the appearance of the mediator and his or her office staff is extremely important. Their appearance and demeanor should match the office. Clothing, hairstyles, and manner should be businesslike, refined, tasteful and low-key. The ideal office personality might be described in the same terms.

It is important to note that this elitism, which may be conveyed, should only be implied, never stated. There never should be any nonverbal or verbal communication that divorce mediation is only for the affluent. The suggestion being made is simply that these are the sort of people who have the intelligence and good sense to see mediation's benefits and put them to use in their own lives.

This old-fashioned, stable office surrounding, although subtle, has great import. It's very familiar, from media images seen in the past, and it also gives the consumer a sense of safety and security. The Kindred Spirits Study noted how particularly relevant this was for the majority of men and women.

Finally, this office image is highly reminiscent of the sort of office that might be found at a very traditional established law firm. Psychologically, in the prospective consumer's mind, a connection between mediation and the legal system may be made.

## Environment

As any person, who has ever been forced to shop for a last-minute gift after a difficult work day, realizes, environment can affect decisions. Formal research shows that environment can affect a consumer's attitude toward shopping. Furthermore, attempts to influence environment by advertising run into something of a Catch 22. Advertisements designed to create an environment work only when the consumer is already in a positive, or, at least, neutral mood (Gardner 1985).

The implications of this research are not particularly good for divorce mediation. It can be safely assumed that at least one of the parties involved in a divorce, and perhaps both, are in an on-going, bad mood during this period.

This knowledge, then, reiterates the importance of two aforementioned points. One is the need to reach prospective consumers and build their awareness of mediation long before they have begun to consider divorce. The second is the need for media exposure as widespread as budget will allow. The greater number of media impressions that reach the prospective divorcee, the more likely he or she will be influenced while in a receptive mood.

## Dominant culture in the United States

There has been a great deal of research about cultural influences in other nations, and about subcultural influences in the United States.

Black female consumers as a group, for instance, may have different concepts of beauty and may react differently to hair care and coloring products than do white female consumers. Teenage consumers are more likely to respond to certain kinds of appeals than are senior citizens and vice versa. Urban and rural consumers often exhibit different values and lifestyles.

Perhaps, it may be that we give too little thought to the ways that American consumers are different. We are so close to our own culture, and so rarely exposed firsthand to that of other nations that we may take some of our own values for granted - both as consumers and as marketers.

It has been suggested that relevant cultural values can be identified in terms of six bipolar dimensions. Cultures are either egalitarian or elitist, performance-oriented or tradition-oriented, materialistic or nonmaterialistic, objective or subjective, intensive (mechanistic) or extensive (holistic), and individualistic or collectivistic (Lipset 1963).

Beginning with this theory and expanding on it, American culture in the late twentieth century can be described in the following seven categories. We are:

- evaluative and moralistic
- humanistic and egalitarian

We are in favor of:

- human mastery over nature/human perfectibility
- materialism and progress
- individualism and achievement
- time orientation
- youthfulness

Several of these points should be considered for the public relations campaign of divorce mediation.


## The Role and Nature of Social Power

How can mediators influence the decisions of prospective clients? It happens in much the same way that friends, relatives, and passers-by influence each other.

People have the power to influence the behavior of others. The sources of such power fall into one or more of five categories: coercive, legitimate, reward, referent and expert power (French and Raven 1959).

Neither coercive power ("Buy it, or you'll die"; "Buy It, or you'll look bad") nor so-called legitimate power ("Buy it because it's the American way") is as relevant to the divorce mediators as the other three categories.

Reward power can have two forms. It may be the ability to give material rewards, such as money or privileges, or it may take the form of psychological reward, such as recognition and

praise. The advertising message from a sweepstakes company -
"enter before December 31 and you may win $100,000 a year
for the rest of your life" - uses the power of material reward.
(The same message may imply a form of coercive power as well,
if the impression is given that entrants should subscribe to
several magazines on their entry form.) On the other hand, the
ad, which suggests how fulfilling it is to send a monthly check
to a needy child somewhere halfway around the world employs
the power of psychological reward.

As mediators, we have the power of psychological
reward available as a communications tool.    Prospective
consumers must be reminded that studies show that the
successful use of divorce mediation will lead to increased self-
esteem and a sense of competence.   "Try it," the message can
say, albeit in a far more subtle choice of words, "you'll feel
better."

Divorce mediation offers some material reward as well.
Husbands and fathers can be reminded that mediation is more
likely than litigation to result in a custody and visitation
arrangement with which they (the non-custodial parent) will be
happy. "Buy it, and you'll be closer to your kids."

Expert Power is somewhat different and relies, as its
name indicates, on the communicator's expertise, rather than his
or her recognizability.   If a TV star says she takes a particular
brand of pain-killer; then, this is referent power. If a physician
says he or she recommends that brand to patients; this is expert
power.

For divorce mediation, the greatest experts may be
attorneys or judges.   If a respected jurist makes a public
statement about his or her belief in the benefits of divorce
mediation, the consumer is likely to pay special and respectful
attention.   Although Americans may express negative attitudes
toward both the legal profession and the court system, they make
it clear that they consider them sources of the greatest possible
protection and assurance.

## Role Theory and Role Relationships

The late 1980s and 1990s have been hard times for role theory, at least in terms of interpersonal relationships. For decades and perhaps centuries before, almost any American could explain the qualities and duties of a good wife and of a good husband. Those values have been questioned in recent years, however, and the definitions have changed and evolved, at least, in the opinions of some. It appears that no culturally universal definitions exist at this time.

It is even more difficult to define the proper role behavior of an ex-wife or ex-husband. And, it is perhaps even more perplexing to attempt to act out the transitional role of a soon-to-be-former spouse.

Marketers rely on role theory in numerous ways. Some products are purchased particularly to symbolize role relationships. An engagement ring is one example. The purchase of the services of a divorce mediator is another.

The problem is that roles cannot exist and be played unless there are a set of shared expectations about behavior in the relationship. Mediators can put role theory to good use by establishing and communicating appropriate role behaviors for divorcing husbands and wives.

## The power of the Reference Group

There is another kind of expert power, and it may be the most authoritative of all. For a consumer, his or her social group may be recognized as the collective expert. They are the people to whom the consumer listens on issues of norms, values, and even product benefits.

Many successful public relations people have attributed their achievements to simple word-of-mouth. Relatively little research has been done on group influence on consumer behavior, but the studies that have been done indicate enormous power.

People do buy the same products that their friends buy, but it is not, as some might think, a matter of peer pressure. They do it, not in order to comply with group behavior, but in order to get, what they perceive as, a good product. After all, the group must know what they're doing (Burnkrant and Cousineau 1975).

A scene of two housewives exchanging views on brands of laundry detergent or floor waxes in TV commercials is not totally unrealistic.   People at social gatherings do discuss products they like and dislike, and they do so at some length. The process has been dubbed "taste exchange" (Riesman, Glazer and Denney 1950).

The influence of the reference group may, in fact, be greater than that of mass media.  One study presented an index of effectiveness in terms of sources of influence that lead consumers to change product brands.  Personal contacts came out at the top of the list  followed by various, advertising media and salespeople (Katz and Lazarsfeld 1955).  Some researchers, however, question whether a contemporary study would yield the same results.  The research done in 1955 did not take into account the tremendous power of television advertising. Nevertheless, personal contact appears to be of great importance in consumer decisions.

This influence does vary, on the other hand, depending on the product or product classification in question (Witt and Bruce 1972).   Factors that determine influence include the perceived expertise of one's social group, one's need for social approval, and the risk associated with the product. It is difficult to assess the influence of a reference group's influence on divorce mediation without formal research specifically on that question.

Certainly, there is a significant degree of risk associated with the selection of a professional to handle one's divorce.  It also seems likely that friends, who have gone through divorces, would have, for someone divorcing for the first time, a highly perceived degree of expertise.  Further, even a highly confident man or woman might feel a greater need than usual for social approval, while going through a divorce.

Hypothetically, this adds up to a high level of influence for the reference group in terms of decisions made about divorce.  When friends suggest that the prospective divorcee should get a good lawyer, she or he is likely to accept and act on that advice.  And, of course, because in the past so many more people have chosen litigated divorce rather than mediation, the legal alternative is the one far more likely to be recommended.

Divorce mediators may choose to address this issue directly by pointing out to prospective consumers that this is not a time to listen to one's friends, but to make a choice that is personally and individually right for them.  They might also point out that friends making these recommendations may not be particularly happy; in fact, they may not have handled their own divorces in the most constructive ways.  "This is your divorce," the message might convey, "You can do it better."

## Instrumental psychological needs

H.A. Murray also developed a list of psychological needs.  Some are similar to or encompassed by those on Maslow's list, but there are some important differences.  The needs on Murray's list are often referred to as instrumental because they are learned patterns of behavior developed and practiced in order to meet more basic needs.  Some social scientists have pointed out that Murray's basic needs may not be as powerful and motivating as Maslow's.  However, for divorce mediators, Murray's list is more useful since the definitions and solutions are somewhat more specific and, therefore, more accessible.

The twenty needs are as follows: abasement, achievement, affiliation, aggression, autonomy, counteraction, defendence, deference, dominance, exhibition, harm avoidance, inavoidance, nurturance, order, play, rejection, sentience, sex, succorance, and understanding (Murray 1938).  Divorce mediators should pay special attention to at least four of these needs.

Achievement is defined, at least in part, as the need to strive to do something difficult as well as quickly as possible. This elementary ego need could be satisfied by presenting divorce mediation as a challenge, its completion as an important achievement.

Affiliation refers primarily to the formation of friendships and other associations. It may also refer, however, to the need to cooperate with others. Divorce mediation certainly may be positioned as a cooperative venture.

Autonomy, of course, is the need for independence, the desire to resist influence or coercion. Litigated divorce may be looked upon as having great potential for dependence, coercion and influence. Choosing divorce mediation may be presented as an opportunity for the divorcing person to stand on his or her own two feet.

Inavoidance is defined by Murray (1938) as the need to avoid failure, shame, humiliation or ridicule. Although prospective users might feel some fear of failure in approaching divorce mediation, it can be pointed out that there is a far greater possibility of failure in litigated divorce, particularly in the courtroom. The courtroom is a public place in which either of the divorcing parties intentionally may be subjected to humiliation or ridicule by the spouse's attorney. Divorce mediation offers privacy and a more accepting attitude on the part of the professionals in charge.


## Motivational Conflict

Virtually every first-year psychology student has been taught the definitions of the three kinds of motivational conflict: approach-approach, approach-avoidance, and avoidance-avoidance.

An approach-approach conflict is a choice between two attractive alternatives. Should one order the strawberry shortcake or the pecan pie? Should the couple buy the 12-room colonial house or the sprawling ranch-styled house?

An approach-avoidance conflict involves choices that have both attractive and unattractive features. A person might want to have a beautiful body, for instance, but hate to exercise. Or the same person might want to order the aforementioned strawberry shortcake, but realizes that this could mean weight gain and a certain amount of guilt.

An avoidance-avoidance conflict is a choice between unpleasant alternatives. Colloquialisms like "between the devil and the deep blue sea" and "out of the frying pan into the fire" indicate that such conflicts were recognized long before they were given a psychology textbook name.

The decision to divorce can be considered a classic avoidance-avoidance conflict. Either the person continues to live unhappily with the present spouse, or goes through the agonies of the divorce process. Divorcing men and women also may see the choice between mediation and litigation as an avoidance-avoidance conflict. Either they turn their lives over to expensive, unsympathetic, inaccessible attorneys, or they put their trust in less experienced, perhaps less authoritative mediators, who, then, demand that the clients do most of the work themselves.

The challenge for the mediator is to transform one of the negative alternatives into a positive one. In this case, mediators must be seen as more sympathetic and more accessible, and the mediation experience as an opportunity for autonomy, rather than a failure to guide and protect.

## The consumer's self-concept

The goods and services, which consumers choose, are symbols of a consumer's self-concept. The things, which they buy and use, communicate to others how they see themselves, and it becomes crucial that these goods and services enhance the self-concept, rather than detract from or alter it.

A man, who considers himself a wine connoisseur, might be horrified, if someone suggested he purchase an inexpensive jug of wine, for instance. Any adult who considers himself or herself fashionable and upscale might die rather than buy a single item for the new fall wardrobe at a discount store. This behavior accounts for the proliferation of Rolls-Royces, mansions, crystal goblets and elegant interiors seen in advertisements for such unlikely products as mustard, tonic water, TV dinners, and even dog food.

Of course, not every self-concept relates to affluence. People who see themselves as friendly and down-home may be attracted by beer commercials showing friendly gatherings. Almost every possible self-concept can be and has been addressed through persuasive messages.

Keeping this concept in mind, divorce mediators must approach women and men who see themselves already as decent human beings and particularly good mothers and fathers. Messages, which stress the connection between decency, good parenting and mediation, will help keep those particular, positive self-concepts intact.

## Problem-solving theory

One well-accepted theory of decision-making views the consumer as a problem solver, who chooses to buy certain goods and services, because each is seen as the solution to a particular problem. In classic problem-solving theory, the activity involves five stages (Dewey 1910). Modified slightly to reflect consumer behavior, they are as follows:
   -Problem recognition
   -Search for a satisfactory solution
   -Evaluation of alternative solutions
   -Purchase decision
   -Postpurchase evaluation

Perhaps the most relevant features of this theory for the mediators of divorce mediation are the internal information search (during stage two) and the postpurchase evaluation.

Divorce mediation is at a distinct disadvantage during the prospective consumer's internal information search. He or she will think back to what they know, what they've heard, and what they've experienced in terms of divorce. Because of the prevalence of litigated divorce, most of their memory will focus on the use of divorce lawyers, rather than on mediation.

To combat this, the mediators must make it as easy as possible for prospective consumers to remember anything they do hear about divorce mediation. The use of devices like slogans, product symbols and mnemonics may be called for in this effort (Runyon and Stewart 1987).

Consumer satisfaction is a complex phenomenon, which may explain why approximately 20 percent of all purchases produce some dissatisfaction. Because mediation is a service that may be used once and oniy once in a consumer's life (assuming he or she does not go through multiple divorces), it is the satisfaction or dissatisfaction of that consumer's friends and acquaintances, which will influence him or her. Research on the determinants of consumer dissatisfaction is not clear, and there are few guidelines for countering it.

The divorce mediator may want to point out the high level of consumer complaints for all kinds of products and legal services and perhaps, as suggested in the discussion of motivational conflicts, position mediation as the lesser of two evils. After all, it could be said that there is no such thing as a good divorce. The best one can hope for is a somewhat painful but successful one.


## Psychological comfort zones

Consumers differ dramatically in their reactions to what they see or hear and what appeals to them. By plotting assertiveness against emotional responsiveness, a Wilson

Learning Corporation report divided consumers into four social-style categories.  The report then recommended that sales and marketing messages be addressed to each in ways that fall into their "psychological comfort zones."

The four social style categories are as follows:

1) Analyticals:

Motivated by logic, rather than emotion.

Respond best to a familiar, predictable environment.

**Best Appeal:**

Tangible proof, detailed agreements.

Statements made by recognized authorities.

2) Drivers:

Self-motivated.

Like to control others.

**Best Appeal:**

Greater control over time, data, etc.

"It pays for itself."

3) Amiables:

Loyal, dependable team workers.

Good listeners.

Prefer low-pressure situations.

**Best Appeal:**

Emphasis on traditions

Personalized service.

Stress human considerations.

"Trust this not to give you trouble."

4) Expressives:

Thrive on people contact.

Look for short-term results.

Like to be noticed.

Seekers of approval.

**Best Appeal:**

Testimonials.

"This is for the winners."

(Ingrasci 1981)

Because all four social-style types are likely to be found among prospective consumers for divorce mediation, it is good news that the messages proposed so far should appeal in at least one way to each type.

Pro-mediation statements made by attorneys and judges should appeal to analyticals, as will the fact that the mediation process includes the drafting of a detailed agreement.

Drivers will appreciate the amount of control over the divorce process and the low rate of post-divorce custody and visitation problems, as well as with its people-oriented approach. The stress on its long historical and cultural tradition also should be appealing.

For expressives, the concept of "successful divorce" should be effective.

The amiables are the most likely to be open to the concept and process of mediation. At least three of its most important  points are believed to appeal to the amiables' psychology.

## Attitudes and Attitude Change

Before any mediator can determine how and when a consumer's attitude can be changed, he or she must know why the consumer has this particular attitude to begin with. The consumer's motivation is crucial.

Attitudes are said to serve one of four purposes: adjustment, ego defense, value expression or knowledge.

Adjustment attitudes exist to help us receive rewards or avoid punishment, and are often involved in group membership. Students at a particular school, members of a certain team or workers in a specific occupation hold attitudes that are very likely to change after leaving the school, team or career field. A college professor transferred to a new campus, who lets emotional ties to his last place of work fade away and develops loyalties to the new campus, has experienced such an attitude change.

Adjustment-based attitudes tend to change only when past satisfactions are no longer forthcoming, or when one's aspirations are raised. Ego-defensive attitudes include the use of projection, compensation and rationalization. Normally, these attitudes are held at such a complex and deeply psychological level that there is little that can be done to alter them. They are best left to mental health professionals.

A value-expressive attitude held by a consumer reflects the central values that he or she holds dear. A smoker may continue to buy and use cigarettes, for instance, because smoking represents adulthood and/or sophistication for him or her. The hard facts about health risks connected with smoking are relatively impotent, compared with the emotional power of this value.

The divorce mediator is unlikely to alter the basic values of any individual man or woman, much less an entire culture. The most effective strategy when dealing with value-expressive attitudes is to align with them instead. Identify with prevalent values and surround your service with symbols that reflect them.

Knowledge is the motivation for another class of attitudes which help us understand and organize an all too complicated world. Generalizations and stereotypes fall into this category. Certain consumers may choose to believe that all lawyers are scoundrels, for instance, or conversely that all lawyers are extremely intelligent. To hold such an attitude demands far less thought, energy and consideration than carefully and individually judging each lawyer that one meets or hears about.

A problem for mediators is that consumers holding knowledge-function attitudes evaluate and make judgements about what are and are not appropriate forms of distribution, promotion and the like. Some might decide, for instance, that lawyers shouldn't advertise. And some might strongly believe that divorce shouldn't be handled by non-lawyers.

Attitude change is the primary goal of public relations strategy, of course. Three important Public Relations theories on attitudes and how they can be changed: Cognitive consistency theory, Information Processing and Reasoned Action theory.

The Cognitive Consistency theory holds that, when new information is introduced to a person, this creates an inconsistency that forces the components of the particular attitude out of balance. This creates a tension that the person feels compelled to resolve. He or she may resolve it by responding in one of two ways: discrediting the new information altogether, or modifying the original attitude.

A person who believes that divorce negotiations should never be handled by non-lawyers, for instance, might be informed that studies show negotiations handled with a divorce mediator result in fewer custody and visitation problems than in litigated divorce. This person might simply dismiss the new information by saying or thinking, "I don't believe that's true" or "Who did that study? You can make statistics show anything." Or that person might stop and think, "Really? Well, I didn't realize that agreements with mediators turned out so well. I never would have thought that."

Mediators may use any of three strategies to introduce such new information. These strategies might be summarized as the consumer rule for the Cognitive Consistency theory: inform, tempt or seduce. That is, the use of informational ads, brochures or other messages, may tempt the consumer to try the new product or service by means of sales, free samples, money-saving coupons or demonstrations, or ads and other messages in emotional formats designed to change the consumer's feelings about the service may also be tried.

Information processing may well be the most widely used attitude change theory in public relations. According to this theory, there are six steps to obtaining a response to any communication: presentation of the message, attention to the message, comprehension of the conclusion (and arguments), yielding to the conclusion, retention of the belief, and finally behaving on the basis of the new belief.

Information Processing theory stresses the importance of getting the consumer's attention. This is why the first few seconds of a TV or radio ad are considered crucial. The same is true of the headlines and leads of messages in print.

Because the consumer must be able to easily understand the message and see its relevance to his or her situation, the so-called slice-of-life format is commonly used in ads and other messages. Certainly, the divorce mediators can benefit from presenting what might be referred to as "scenes from a divorce" in ads, brochures, and other communications.

Finally, the consumer must remember the message until he or she has an opportunity to act on it. This is particularly important for behavioral changes because, as stated earlier, mediation's consumers must be reached and persuaded long before they set the steps of divorce in motion. Recall is best when the message is particularly persuasive and when frequency of exposure is high. A plan for heavy media exposure is in keeping with these principles.

The theory of Reasoned Action places great importance on the subjective norm, which is what a consumer believes relevant. The subjective norm is what the consumer thinks that others think about his or her actions or thoughts. One study showed that consumers' beliefs about what others think of a particular behavior strongly influenced a seemingly mundane practice such as clipping and using product coupons to the extent that they stopped clipping coupons (Shimp and Kavas 1984).

This complex picture of consumer behavior is of enormous relevance to public relations. If a consumer really would like to buy a BMW but does not do so because he believes that family, neighbors, or business associates might view his choice unfavorably, then the auto manufacturer has accomplished little in persuading the individual.

Divorce mediation would appear to be particularly susceptible to the dangers inherent in this integrated theory of attitude change and reference group influence. Mediators may convince Jane Doe of the benefits of divorce mediation over litigated divorce, but if her friends, who have gone through divorces in the past, disapprove of divorce mediation, or if she believes they might, she may well decide against mediation. If friends or family members urge her to get a powerful attorney, who will teach her soon-to-be ex-husband a lesson, she may (because she believes these friends or relatives to be experts in many ways) yield to their preferences.

A variation on this concept is Cooperative Decision-making. Both husband and wife must decide to go into mediation; if one agrees and the other balks, they are most likely to fall back on the traditional solution of hiring two attorneys and fighting things out.

Cooperative decision-making is a challenge to mediators in any situation. For example, a husband and wife must agree on whether Disney World, a week at the beach, or a visit to the historic sites in New England would be the best possible vacation this year. Unless they both decide on a destination, both lose. It is especially difficult in divorce mediation since it demands cooperative decision-making at a time when cooperation is antithetical to the situation.

A strategy that has been found effective in very difficult cases is to associate the new product with the preferred brand, rather than selling directly against it. The Ford Motor Company used this strategy in introducing the Thunderbird. An advertising headline, "Now there are three great American cars," linked the new car with the Cadillac and the Lincoln Continental, positioning all three as the ultimate in luxury automobiles.

This strategy is in keeping with the research that indicates a strong need to link divorce mediation with the legal and court systems because of the latter's widespread image of strength and consumer or client protection. Then, when a well-meaning friend or relative says, "Don't take any chances. Get yourself a good lawyer." The divorcing man or woman can answer, "Yes, I'm going to. I'm using a top mediator who is associated with a top law firm or lawyer.

## Elements of persuasive communication

Messages are most likely to be persuasive when three qualifications are met: the source of the communication has high credibility; there is a similarity between the source and the receiver; and the conclusions are explicit, rather than implicit.

For the prospective consumer of divorce mediation, then, the source of the message must be someone considered an expert in divorce (most likely a judge, divorce attorney or a celebrity with high general credibility). The man or woman receiving the message must see the expert as similar to him or her in some way. Therefore, it is ideal that both women and men be used as spokespeople and that they be members of the age group in which divorces are most likely to occur. Actors and "real people" ages 35-45, part of the first wave of the baby boom generation, are recommended. Finally, the message must spell it out for the viewer, listener or reader. The message must not only indicate why divorce mediation is a good decision, but tell them outright that this is so.

## Summary

This analysis of important, persuasive concepts has both reiterated the importance of certain aforementioned strategies and yielded new insights into tactics that can be effective in social change. These concepts provide new guidance, particularly in terms of the style of the ideal message. Recommendations are as follows:

- Media images of divorce mediation offices should reflect traditional, civilized, old-money luxury.
- The slice-of-life format or "scenes from a divorce" will help make the message relevant and easily understood, based on the Information Processing theory.
- Slogans, symbols and mnemonics should be employed to make the divorce mediation message easy to remember.

- Informational approaches will be useful,
  according to the Cognitive Consistency theory
  of attitude change.
- Emotional and seductive approaches will be
  useful, according to the same principles.
- In both kinds of messages, the conclusion
  should be spelled out for the prospective
  consumer: Divorce mediation is a good idea;
  divorce mediation is the way to go.
- Testimonials by attorneys and/or judges are
  recommended as an effective use of expert
  power.
- Spokespeople should be, or appear to be,
  members of the baby boom generation,
  approximately 35-45 years of age at this time.
- Both male and female spokespeople should be
  used.

The analysis of these concepts also has revealed a wider market segment than might have been assumed. In fact, prospective consumers must include male and female adults of all ages and of every marital status.

The decision to use divorce mediation is likely to be made only after long term and repeated exposure to the concept and its advantages. Therefore, all married people ideally should hear about mediation for years. Then, when they are about to divorce and likely to make a quick decision, they will be pre-sold on the idea. This is also advisable because people leading normal, relatively calm lives are more receptive to new ideas than people in emotional turmoil.

The target population must also be broadened to include anybody who is likely to be part of the divorcing couple's reference group. According to the theory of Reasoned Action, they will be consulted on divorce-related decisions and their opinions will carry a great deal of weight. This segment must be regarded as enormous in number because it must include anyone who is now or ever will be a relative, friend or associate of any man or woman who may someday go through a divorce.

At the same time that the reference group is courted by mediators, the group's importance can also be minimized in messages directed at the prospective consumer. A communication message designed to reduce the reference group's power might be phrased in this way: "Sure, this is a difficult time. And you're going to seek out the advice of people you care about. Listen to them. You need friends at a time like this. But remember this is your divorce, not theirs. Maybe you can do things better."

If divorce mediation must target more specific groups, then the focus should be on the urban and suburban middle-class to upper-middle-class adults. Studies to date show that they are more likely to use private mediation services.

The analysis of media concepts reiterates the importance of an intensive and on-going media campaign. According to Information Processing theory, frequency of impressions is an important factor for persuasion and attitude change.

What we learn about the message itself might be summarized in these terms:

- Mediation will make you a better person (as people throughout the world and in other cultures have long realized).
- With mediation, you'll feel better about yourself.
- With mediation, you'll be a success.
- With mediation, things will work out better in practical terms.

The emphasis on a message that the use of divorce mediation makes one a better person -- or indicates that someone would choose it because he or she is inherently a better person -- has at least four special sources of appeal.

It complements the American values of egalitarianism and humanism by putting the personal concerns and feelings of individual human beings before the dictates of impersonal courts and laws. It also reflects the American belief that human beings are indeed perfectible. The user of mediation strives to be a good human being and perfect parent. The same message also reinforces the self-concepts of those who believe themselves to be good human beings and good parents.

The message, furthermore, appeals to what some social scientists refer to as "the amiables," who look favorably on appeals which emphasize human considerations and person-centered approaches, as well as historical and cultural traditions.

The second facet of the message - that the use of mediation leads to a consumer feeling better about himself or herself - has several psychological bases. The message is in itself a use of reward power, promising consumers that, when they choose divorce mediation, they will reap psychological rewards such as heightened self-esteem and an increased sense of competence.

Divorce mediation also may be presented as a means of fulfilling affiliation needs (cooperation with spouse and mediator), autonomy needs (designing the divorce agreement oneself rather than turning the task over to lawyers) and inavoidance needs (dealing with issues in private, rather than facing the possible humiliation in court and the possibility of failure, which exists when approaching divorce from a win-or-lose point of view).

Psychologically, consumers also will feel better about themselves because they will be taught the rules of behavior for their new roles as ex-husbands and ex-wives. With these shared expectations, both parties will feel more secure psychologically and are likely to come to terms more comfortably with life after divorce. A feeling of psychological safety also is likely to result from the association of divorce mediation with the legal system.

"With mediation, you'll be a success," stresses the recurring importance of successful divorce. It complements the American value of love of achievement and presents divorce mediation as a challenge which will enable the consumer to meet instrumental achievement needs.

It is also important to present mediation in practical terms. Because we are a nation of clock-watchers, its time-saving function reflects the American value of time management. This is a persuasive selling point.

Its much higher success rate and much lower problem rate in terms of child custody and visitation agreements have practical appeal on at least two levels. The implication that mediation is a process that gives its user very little or no trouble is of particular appeal to the Amiables. And to most would-be-consumers, the likelihood of custody and visitation success is a material reward as well. In this way, the marketing appeal is a use of reward power.

There is a classic, public relations story, told in classroom after classroom. A passenger train company spent millions of dollars on developing and implementing a huge campaign, which would reach most Americans with numerous media impressions. It was to be an unprecedented effort in terms of market saturation. American people were told about the incredible trains that belonged to this company, the engineering feats that made them possible and the technical marvels that made them run. The campaign failed miserably. People showed no indication of booking more train trips than before.

A public relations expert was approached, and he pointed out the company's mistake. "You've done a wonderful job of selling your trains to the American public," he explained. "But that's just the problem. You're not selling trains. You're selling vacations. At least you're supposed to be."

Because the average, American consumer was unlikely to purchase a passenger train for his or her own use, the campaign had been meaningless. A second campaign, which emphasized comfort, relaxation, meal service, courtesy scheduling, convenience and the experience of train travel, was launched. When the company realized that what they were selling (i.e., what the consumer would be buying) was travel, it made all the difference.

Mediators must keep in mind that they are divorce mediators. Rather than attempting to paint a picture of a positive divorce experience, it is advisable to make a realistic evaluation of mediation - one that is far more likely to be credible to the intelligent consumer than making divorce sound like a positive action.

# CHAPTER 4

## Public Relations: A Strategy for Persuasion

Divorce mediators must keep in mind that they are selling divorce, and that no one wants to go through a divorce. In most cases, the same consumer who doesn't want to go through all the unpleasantness of a divorce action also doesn't want to stay unhappily married. This is another variation of the aforementioned avoidance-avoidance conflict. How does a mediator give the consumers what they want when they don't want either alternative?

The perfect divorce, as Blades (1984) has suggested, costs nothing and hurts no one. The couple remains good friends, no children are involved and the ex-spouses part a little older but far wiser because of their experience together. Reality rarely lives up to this ideal, but it is important to keep the ideal in mind.

Perhaps, if the mediator could give these hypothetical consumers what they really want, then, they would magically change history and efface their marriage. The millions of women and men who have said or thought, "I should never have married him/her," are expressing the wish for the only truly desirable alternative in such a situation.

The closest thing in reality to that wish is a chance to start over, to begin again with a clean slate. And in some ways, this can be presented as a possibility to men and women about to divorce. Such couples may be ending one relationship with each other, but they are beginning another - that of ex-spouse.

The relationships between ex-husbands and ex-wives have been given relatively little attention in either the academic or popular psychological literature, but they often are real and lasting connections. At least this is true when children are involved.

The largest number of people, who will partake in serial monogamy, and the target market of this public relations program is the post World War II baby boom generation. Defined as those Americans born between 1946 and 1962, they have been described as the generation of later marriage, less marriage, more divorce and fewer children (Jones 1981).

If these are divorce mediation's prime clients, what are they doing? For one thing, they are aging. The baby boomers have already turned 40. In the year 2000, the so-called baby boomers will be defined as those age 38 to 54. At that point, the eldest among them will become part of the second most talked-about market group in the U.S., the senior citizen.

The 55- to 64-year old market is already considered the most affluent consumer market in the country today. When baby boomers and the over-55 market merge, the impact will be enormous. It can be assumed that the baby boomers are similar in, at least, one way to all the middle-aged generations before them. They would love to have their youth back.

Perhaps a lifetime of getting divorced and remarried can be viewed as one attempt to stay young forever. If one is a bride at 45, and manages to look attractive and reasonably youthful, thanks to diet and regular exercise, then one still can feel as if she is just on the brink of adult life. If couples are having children in their 40s and even 50s, then this cannot be middle age -- at least not by its old-fashioned definitions.

At the same time, the baby boomers cannot ignore a growing sense of their own mortality, and some uneasiness with constant change. Approaching middle age often means both a yearning and a need for continuity. To be bound for life, even though divorced, can be viewed as a comfort in many ways.

If divorce mediation were a tangible consumer product, it might be repackaged with a photograph of an aging, but attractive couple on the front, and a brightly-colored banner, reading "New and Improved Fresh-Start Formula: Starting Over as Ex-Spouses." But the marketing of professional services can be neither as simple nor as direct as that of packaged goods, even if the emotional needs of the consumer of the service are as strong or stronger.

Making changes in a service are less clear-cut than in a product since they are far less easily controlled. The analogy is still useful for purposes of clarity. Generally, when manufacturers want to change their product, they will work on four areas: the name, their formula, distribution, and price. For divorce mediation, these changes are a good outline. However, they may not be useful in all cases.

The name, Divorce Mediation, is not particularly ideal; it is often misunderstood and leads prospective clients to believe that it is a pacifistic process that is out of date in the late 1990s. However, no other term describes the process quite as accurately.

Third-party negotiation is the term that comes closest, and might be used as an additional description. With eight syllables, however, it is somewhat unwieldy. The use of a shorthand term, such as "DM" (for divorce mediation) or "TPN" for (third party negotiation), could reek of trendiness and seems at odds with the traditional and conservative media image, which is to be conveyed.

Despite its limitations, the name divorce mediation probably should be retained. Professional education will be employed to correct common misconceptions about it.

In the case of divorce mediation, consistency and quality control, part of the formula, are the most important factors in the actual service provided. It is crucial that divorce mediation be offered as just that and that confusion between it and other services such as therapy, divorce counseling and even arbitration be countered.

The best outlet for distribution of divorce mediation is the law firm. In the ideal situation, one or more mediators would be employed full-time as staff members of each of the thousands of law firms across the country and would work out of the firms' offices. Clients might come to mediators on direct personal recommendation, or they might approach the law firm first and be assigned to a staff mediator. This method and setting of distribution can add immeasurably to both the prestige and credibility of the mediation service and practitioner.

Divorce mediation is or should be a valuable service performed by highly trained and skilled professionals. Its price structure should reflect the expertise of its practitioners. Therefore, it is recommended that, divorce mediators charge a fee structure by the hour and based on experience, skills and reputation. Just as there always have been higher-priced lawyers, there should be both expensive and inexpensive divorce mediators.

## Changing Consumer Behavior

The proposed public relations plan for divorce mediation will target three important audiences: the general consumer, the legal profession, and the mental health professions.

By far, the most important audience is the general consumer because overall public acceptance of mediation is absolutely necessary to its success. In addition, those whom we wish to reach - the attorneys, judges, psychiatrists, psychologists, psychotherapists, social workers, marriage and family counselors - can be included in the general public and can be further reached through professionally oriented media.

A number of major media should be employed in this public relations effort such as television, talk shows, television news programs, radio advertising, television advertising, radio talk show. The first proposed campaign, "There Is Such a Thing as a Good Divorce," is appropriate for television spots, radio spots and magazine ads. They should be supplemented by a free booklet offered to viewers and readers.

## Scripts for Radio and Television

**There Is Such a Thing as a Good Divorce**

Spot #1: "Real Woman" (01:00)

(Extreme close up of attractive, sophisticated woman in her mid to late 30s. Her facial expression is serious. She seems calm and speaks in a quiet, almost confidential voice.)

Woman:          There is such a thing as a good divorce; let me tell you. Especially when you have children.

                    David and I made up our minds, as soon as we knew there was really no saving this marriage. We decided that, whatever our problems were, our kids weren't going to be dragged into court. And they weren't going to see us treating each other like - well, you know, the way so many people do when they're out for blood.

                    Oh, I was angry. Trust me. I didn't like seeing my whole life turned upside down. But David and I decided to be civilized about this. Or at least as civilized as we could.

                    We asked our lawyer about Mediation. And that's the way we did it. By talking things out with the Mediator, we came to an agreement about custody, visitation, everything.

                    It wasn't fun, but we worked it out. And even if our Marriage is over, we've got the rest of our lives to be parents to our kids. Good parents. And we're not going to let a divorce ruin this.

Voice over:     Divorce mediation. There is such a thing as a good divorce.

Spot #2: "Real Man" (01:00)

(Extreme close up of attractive man in his mid to late 30s.  He is serious and has a calm demeanor.)

Man:      There is such a thing as a good divorce.  And I should know because I've been there.  Twice.

          But at least I've learned from my mistakes.  The first time around, Kathy and I almost came to blows in her lawyer's office.  And I was afraid for a while that I'd never see my son again.  I will never forget the look in his eyes the day of that obscene custody hearing.

          This time, it was Barbara and me, and we used Mediation.  I didn't know how much better it would be than doing it the old-fashioned way.  But I knew it couldn't be worse.

          Thank God we did it that way.  I can't say it was fun.  There were some rough moments, but at least it was civilized.  And I'm much happier with the visitation arrangements I have with my daughters.

          People don't realize; divorce may end your marriage, but you still have a bond for life.  I don't ever plan to stop being a father.

Voice over:  Divorce Mediation.  There is such a thing as a good divorce.

Spot #3: "Lawyer" (01:00)

(Extreme close up of attractive male attorney in his 30s or 40s. His facial expression is serious. In fact, he looks a little fed up with something. His voice reveals a bit of that contempt, but his eyes are somewhat sad.)

Attorney:          I don't know why I became a divorce lawyer. But I know it wasn't to watch decent people turn into monsters, or to see kids turn against their parents.

(Slide appears with attorney's name and professional identification)

I believe in the legal system. There's a place for adversarial law. But it isn't for divorce cases.

Maybe if I believed marriage was a game, I'd feel better about seeing a winner and a loser at the end of it. But I don't.

I can tell you how most people feel about someone they've beaten in a lawsuit, or someone they've been beaten by. They never want to see the bum again. That's just great, unless the bum happens to be the mother or father of your children.

There is a better way to handle a divorce. It's called Divorce Mediation. It's civilized. It's sane. It's fair. Lots of lawyers do it now. Lots of others will send you to someone who does.

Voice over:          Divorce mediation. There is such a thing as a good divorce.

Final slide:          A message from .....

Spot #4: "Judge"

(Extreme close up of a distinguished looking judge in his 60s or older. He speaks seriously with authority and compassion.)

Judge: I can't tell you how many divorces I've presided over during my career. I know that I've never seen a good one. And I know that I've seen all too many children in my court. Not kids in trouble, but nice, normal, healthy kids who are there because their parents decided to take each other for everything they had. Financially and emotionally.

I'd like to see everyone of them in divorce Mediation instead. Talking out a settlement. Coming to a fair agreement privately like civilized adults. Private lives don't belong in public courtrooms.

Some states mandate mediation for divorcing couples. All the research shows that people are happier with mediated agreements, happier with the custody and visitation arrangements that come out of them.

Plus it empties out my court so that we can deal with the real criminals. Divorce is not a crime. Mediation is an old idea whose time has come again.

Voice over:     Divorce mediation. There is such a thing as a good divorce.

Final slide:     A message from .......

## Print Ads

Print Ad #1: "Real Woman"

(Full page black and white ad with small head and shoulders photograph of the same woman who appears in television "Real Woman" spot. Again her expression is serious but calm. This will be a heavy-typed informational ad; the following copy will appear below the photograph.)

## "THERE IS SUCH A THING AS A GOOD DIVORCE"

"But don't let anyone try to tell you that divorce will never affect you. Lots of reasonably happy marriages, the kind that would have lasted a lifetime if they had happened a century ago, end up in divorce. And millions of children have to live through it.

"I look on divorce as a fact of modern life. My own parents had been through it. Many of my friends are divorced. So when I realized that David and I couldn't live together anymore, I was able to accept it and try to make the best of a terrible situation.

"We were determined to do things the civilized way. So we asked our lawyer about mediation. His firm assigned us to one of their divorce mediators. He met with us four times and helped us work out the financial side of the divorce as well as the custody and visitation agreement. The remarkable thing is that both David and I are pleased with the results.

"I'll admit I was concerned at first about being 'unprotected' in mediation. Over ten years of marriage, I almost never got equal time in any argument. David is simply a better fighter and a better negotiator than I. He has a lot more experience at it. So I gave some thought to hiring the most expensive bomber divorce lawyer in town so that he could stand up to David on my behalf.

"I'm glad now that I didn't.  First of all, I didn't want to put our children through the ordeal of a custody suit.  And to be quite honest, I didn't like the idea of discussing my personal life in a public courtroom.

"Luckily mediation became a sort of protection for me.  A good mediator considers it his or her first responsibility to balance the negotiations between a husband and wife to be sure that each person gets equal air time.  That certainly hadn't been true in everyday life.  And studies show that women tend to get a raw deal in the courtroom as well.  So, having someone monitor the communications meant a great deal to me.

"It's over now.  Thanks to mediation, it was faster than a litigated divorce would have been.

"We saved money on legal fees too, although that was hardly our most important concern.

"I honestly believe my relationship with David is better than ever.  We make very good ex-spouses.  The kids are doing fine, which is really what matters.  David's going to be their father for the rest of their life.  And I believe that part of being a good mother means letting him stay close to them.

"I think we have one of the most successful divorces in town."

A message from ....

For a free booklet on Marriage, Divorce and Mediation write_____ or call _____.

Print Ad #2: "Real Man"

(Full page black and white ad with small photograph of the same man who appears in the "Real Man" television ad. His expression is serious, thoughtful and calm. The following copy appears beneath the photograph.)


## THERE IS SUCH A THING AS A GOOD DIVORCE

"I'm an expert at it. I'm 42 years old and I've been through it twice.

"But no one can accuse me of not learning from experience. And one thing I've learned is that no matter how much times have changed, women still get custody of the kids.

"I can live with that. I know that both my ex-wives are good mothers. But I won't put up with an agreement that doesn't give me the visitation rights I deserve, and a schedule that's convenient for me and the kids as well as for her. That's why the second time around, I wanted to go for divorce mediation instead of litigation. I don't want to be dictated to by a total stranger, no matter how good an attorney he or she is. This is my personal life, and I don't plan to turn it over to the legal system to run.

"What are divorces doing in courtrooms anyway? We didn't break any laws. We just made a mistake, and now we want to set things right with as little pain and difficulty as possible.

"I've read about some of the studies, and I believe what they say. Mediation gets you to a settlement faster and cheaper. And it leaves you with an agreement that both of you can live with. People who see mediation through very rarely end up back in court. They stick to their agreements because they had a hand in them.

"I know people who have been divorced for ten years, and they're still boiling mad at their ex-spouses. I ask myself sometimes what effect that kind of anger must have on their children. With mediation, Barbara and I were able to talk things out. And once in a while, we actually see each other's point of view.

"No, it's not like therapy or counseling. We had tried that too, but what we learned from it was how incompatible we really were. Mediation is more like labor-management arbitration, except the two of you make the decisions. And it isn't binding until you make it part of the formal divorce agreement.

"At this point in time, I think you have to view divorce as a normal occurrence. Almost everybody goes through it. God knows I don't recommend it, but it doesn't even have to be thought of as a failure. Partnerships break up all the time. The fact that they do doesn't wipe out all the good things that came of them.

"But an ex-wife isn't like an ex-business partner. Our mediator suggested that we think of ex-spouses as a whole new role, a whole new stage in life. I must say we're better at this than we were at being married. As a result, the kids haven't been traumatized and we're still doing our best to be good parents to them.

"I think we have one of the most successful divorces in town."


A message from .....

For a free booklet on Marriage, Divorce and Mediation write _____ or call _____.

Print Ad #3: "Lawyer"

(Full page black and white ad with small photograph of the same male attorney who appeared in the "Lawyer" television ad. He is dressed in a business suit and has a serious expression on his face. The following copy appears beneath the photograph.

## THERE IS SUCH A THING AS A GOOD DIVORCE

"I ought to know. I've been a divorce lawyer for __ years.

"I think there are times when divorce does belong in the courts for instance, when a spouse has suffered abuse. Maybe all divorces belonged in the courts in the 19th century when no self-respecting man or woman would bring shame on the family name by ending a marriage, unless some true horror had been committed.

"But that's hardly true today. Most divorcing couples are just nice people who aren't happy being married any longer. Many times, a term like incompatibility or irreconcilable differences really hits the nail on the head. So why on earth should two law-abiding citizens be forced to end their marriage by litigation?

"Some couples have told me they feel like criminals, being asked to testify in court. Others tell me they're just plain embarrassed to be discussing personal matters in a public forum. More men and women than I'd care to count have realized too late what this ordeal was doing to their children.

"Kids are accustomed to, what some of us still refer to, as 'broken homes.' A lot of them can adapt to divorce faster than we realize. What really hurts them is seeing hate between their parents. And that's the kind of animosity that some litigated divorces help to build.

"You can't blame the lawyers completely.  As jurists, our training is in the practice of adversary law.  And we do this to the best of our abilities.

"But in the last decade or so, some lawyers have taken an unorthodox step, one that is humane as well as practical.  They have begun to practice divorce mediation or to refer clients to other professionals who do.  The American Bar Association has set up standards for its practice.

"Mediation is a practical and useful choice for divorcing couples who are willing to try it.  The husband and wife make their own decisions about financial settlements, custody, visitation and other divorce-related issues.  The mediator is there only to be sure that the negotiation is balanced and fair, and to urge the process forward whenever there are stumbling blocks.

"Mediation is no picnic.  There are moments of anxiety, frustration, resentment and danger.  But those moments are private, and they are a necessary part of working out a fair divorce agreement.  When mediation works - and it does more often than not - the couple's post-divorce relationship is far better than it probably would have been after a court battle.

"I've seen it lead to some of the most successful divorces in town."

A message from .......

For a free booklet on Marriage, Divorce and Mediation write to _____ or call _____.

NOTE: Copy must be approved by the attorney chosen to be the spokesperson for this campaign.  This version should be presented to the spokesperson under consideration, then rewritten to reflect the particular viewpoint of that person.

Print Ad #4: "Judge"

(Full page black and white ad with small photograph of the same judge who appeared in the "Judge" television ads. He is dressed in judicial robes and has a serious, somewhat saddened expression on his face. The following copy appears beneath the photograph.)

## THERE IS SUCH A THING AS A GOOD DIVORCE

"I ought to know. I've presided over more than __ of them.

"I look down at these decent, well-meaning men and women, and I wonder what on earth they're doing in my courtroom. Even more, what are their sons and daughters doing there?

"One thing should be clear to everybody. Getting a divorce isn't a crime. And two unhappy people, who are separating, but who will be bound to each other for life through their children, are only going to make things worse by hurling accusations at each other across a public courtroom.

"That's one reason why I've formally spoken out in favor of divorce mediation. When I am put in charge of deciding a divorce agreement, I have to do it by the book. I have to consider only the laws of the land. When a divorcing husband and wife retain control by working out an agreement with the help of a mediator, they all can consider personal needs and wishes as well. And in cases of personal status such as divorce, this will more likely lead to true justice.

"Mediation is not for everyone. It takes two spouses willing to cooperate at a time of great emotional strain. It's unfortunate that not every couple can take advantage of mediation, however, because its results are quite impressive.

"Couples, who use divorce mediation, reach an agreement more quickly. They are more likely to live up to the terms of their agreement and consider themselves happier with the outcome than couples who pursue the traditional course of litigated divorce. Non-custodial parents report that they are happier with the custody and visitation arrangements decided on through mediation. There are fewer cases of non-payment in mediated custody agreements than in those that are litigated.

"And while many couples consider that their already disintegrating relationships become worse in court, a great many couples, who go through mediation, find that the process actually has improved their relationships. This is not intended as a plea for spouses to reconcile, but for them to be better ex-spouses, if only for the sake of their children.

"I urge couples, who have made the decision to divorce, to consider mediation. The American Bar Association has set up standards for its practice. Mediation is a practice steeped in tradition from biblical days to America's own century-old experience with it in labor-management relations. Applied to family relations, it can lead to extremely successful divorces."


A message from ......

For a free booklet on Marriage, Divorce and Mediation write to
_____ or call _____.


NOTE: Copy must be approved by the judge chosen to be the spokesperson for this campaign. This version should be presented to the spokesperson under consideration, then rewritten to reflect the particular viewpoint of that person. Former Chief Justice Warren E. Burger has spoken out in favor of mediation and would be the ideal choice - should he be willing to participate.

### Booklet: "Marriage, Divorce and Mediation"

An eight-page booklet "There Is Such a Thing as a Good Divorce" can be offered to interested consumers who write or call. The booklet's purpose will be for consumer education explaining what mediation is and how it can be put to use. It should have a classic, low-key appearance, using a neutral color paper and an all-type format - that is, no photographs or illustrations would be included. In addition to lending dignity to the booklet's serious message, this format will be a factor in controlling printing costs.

A corporate sponsor might be sought for such a booklet. In return, the company assuming the costs of production (design, typography and printing) would have its name, address and a brief message about its work appear in the booklet, perhaps on the inside front cover.

The difficulty of locating a sponsoring company eager to associate itself with a negative issue such as divorce is apparent. Some possibilities might include a woman's or family magazine that often features articles on divorce, a real estate company that benefits from the mobility of a divorcing population or a large moving company that benefits from the same phenomenon. Recommended copy for such a booklet appears on the following pages.

(page 1/cover copy)

Marriage, Divorce And Mediation:
A Guide to Successful Divorce and Lifelong Parenthood

Published by _____

(page 2)
## MARRIAGE AND DIVORCE IN THE REAL WORLD

Going through a divorce is bad enough without all the negative attitudes that still surround it. Perhaps, as the twentieth century draws to a close, Americans no longer think of divorce as an event that shames an entire family. However, we are far from viewing it for what it really is.

For one thing, divorce is not a crime. Yet the vast majority of people who go through it do so by hiring attorneys to find fault with the other party and to seek financial gain through legal means. Many actually end up in court, right next to the thieves, embezzlers and drunk drivers. The advocates of no-fault divorce had hoped to bring an end to this pattern, but it continues.

Divorce is not necessarily a sign of failure. In other centuries, when ending a marriage was an action of last resort - a measure perhaps as extreme as personal bankruptcy today, it made sense for men and women, who divorced, to react with a certain amount of dismay.

If history and literature are to be believed, multitudes of highly imperfect marriages lasted lifetimes, as they were intended to do. Perhaps many of those unions were not completely happy or fulfilling by contemporary standards, but compromises, commitments and arrangements made it possible for them to survive. Those who found it necessary to divorce, despite the sanctions against it, may have had good reason to see themselves as failures of sorts.

Nothing could be further from contemporary truth, however. Divorce is considered an option from the very beginning in the majority of today's marriages.

(page 3)

More than a few sincere friends have been heard to say to a newly-divorced man or woman, "Don't feel bad. The two of you had ten good years together, and these days that's quite an accomplishment." The life pattern even has a widely accepted name: serial monogamy. American culture now allows adults to have several wives or husbands, but only one at a time.

Whether these cultural phenomena are good or bad is a question that only future historians can answer. But they are facts of life, and accepting them is the first step to dealing with them successfully.

There is such a thing as successful divorce, or there should be. If you're already divorced, you know that divorce doesn't end the family; it only reshapes it. If you have children, your roles as mother and father will last a lifetime. Even with divorce as part of the formula, those jobs still can be done well.

(box)

**What Makes a Successful Divorce?**

No one has ever officially defined the term, but the following might be considered some of the elements that go into the best possible kind of divorce.

1. No fault grounds.
2. A fair financial settlement.
3. A custody arrangement acceptable to the non-custodial parent.
4. Child support and other payments faithfully made.
5. Agreement reached over relatively short time period.
6. Reasonable legal fees and other costs.
7. No court trial.
8. Visitation schedule respected for years to come.
9. Ex-spouses able to communicate when future consultations are necessary
10. Self-esteem of both spouses is maintained and fostered.

(page 4)

## Mediation: The Route to Successful Divorce

Achieving successful divorce appears to be more than a matter of luck. Research shows that divorce agreements reached through mediation, rather than through the traditional route of lawyers and litigation result in some very positive benefits. The list includes many of the points that made up the preceding definition of successful divorce itself.

Some of the benefits of divorce mediation compared to litigated divorce:
- Saves time since agreements are reached faster than in litigated divorce.
- Saves money, particularly on legal fees.
- Focuses more on your children's needs and welfare than do court hearings.
- Keeps you both out of court.
- Focuses on your self-determination since you have complete control over yourself and your children's future instead of into the hands of a lawyer.
- Gives both of you opportunities to express your individual points of view on divorce-related issues.
- Keeps the discussions more focused.
- Allows for a more positive agreement on custody-related arrangements.
- Raises self-esteem by taking matters into your own hands.
- It works. Three out of four couples, who enter mediation, have reached satisfactory agreements.

Who says? The first studies done on divorce mediation in the 1980s reported these conclusions. Participants in the study were from the men and women who went through divorces and from practicing mediators.

Divorce mediation is a relatively recent phenomenon, but only because the prevalence of divorce in our society is both recent and unprecedented. Mediation itself has been around for thousands of years.

(page 5)

## How Mediation Works

Mediation is a simple enough idea. Observers like to say that it probably began the first time two cave people had a disagreement and a third happened to be around to help them resolve their dispute.

It has been practiced by religious councils, village elders, international diplomats, neighborhood cops and mothers of toddlers in virtually every corner of the world generation after generation. It has been a reflection of the cultural values of both Japan and China throughout most of recorded Asian history.

Mediation's advocates seem to spend a great deal of time explaining what it is not. Mediation is not therapy. Mediation sessions may touch on you and your spouse's emotional issues, but only as a tool to help clear communications. Divorce mediation is a problem solving process devoted to the present, the future and a couple's behavior. Therapy, on the other hand, will delve into the past for remedial investigation of the couple's situation.

Mediation is also not marriage counseling. It may be viewed as a way to restore harmony. However, it is not an attempt to save a marriage. When you decide to go to a divorce mediator, the decision to end your marriage has already been made. The mediator's object is to help you reach a mutually pleasing arrangement for divorce in a civilized fashion. Reconciliation is never a divorce mediator's goal.

Mediation is not "binding arbitration," a term often heard in the realm of labor-management relations. When an arbitrator is called in to hear both sides of a dispute, his or her decision is final. Before the process begins both parties agree to abide by the arbitrator's decision. However, a divorce mediator makes no decisions about your divorce; you and your spouse do. He or she is there as a professional to guide discussion, balance communication, and assist in breaking through any potential deadlocks.

(page 6)

When you enter mediation, the practitioner you work with will explain the process you are about to undergo. Every professional works differently, of course; but some general guidelines apply to every experience.

You and your spouse will meet the mediator for regularly scheduled sessions at his or her office. The most common session length is an hour or an hour and a half. During these meetings, you will talk out the issues, which the two of you have agreed to have mediated - custody, visitation, child support, property settlement, other financial issues and all matters that will be part of the divorce agreement. Some mediators meet with the husband or wife individually, practicing a kind of shuttle diplomacy. Others prefer that all discussions take place with both spouses present.

When an agreement has been satisfactorily reached, the terms are, then, put on paper. This document is submitted for legal review before becoming the actual divorce agreement.


(box)

FOR MORE INFORMATION

(page 7)

## Q&A: MORE ABOUT MEDIATION

Q: What is wrong with litigated divorce?

A: Ask almost any friend who has been through a litigated divorce, and you're likely to hear that a great deal is wrong with resolving such emotional issues exclusively through the legal system. Some men and women say they feel like criminals. Others have been embarrassed about discussing personal matters in public.

   The legal system exists to resolve questions of right and wrong usually between individuals or organizations who will have no future dealings with each other. Most divorces, on the other hand, are not a matter of wrongdoing; and, furthermore, most ex-spouses still have to maintain some sort of relationship in the future.

   Divorce lawyers actually may stir up hostility and conflict. They don't call it an adversarial system for nothing. Yet the last thing a divorcing man or woman needs is another adversary.


Q: But don't I have to have a lawyer in order to get a divorce?

A: Absolutely. What you may not know is that many divorce mediators are attorneys who have chosen the practice of, what some call, "non-adversarial law." If you choose a mediator with another professional background, perhaps a psychologist or other mental health profession, you simply need to have the mediated agreement reviewed by an attorney. You and your spouse may choose to submit the agreement to separate attorneys, or you may use one attorney jointly. Or, the mediator may work regularly with a lawyer. There are a growing number of lawyer/mediator teams.

(page 8)

Q: Does divorce mediation deal only with child custody? Or can other issues be worked out during the session?

A: Any concrete problem, which arises as a result of the divorce, can be addressed during divorce mediation. Many court-based mediation programs have dealt exclusively with custody issues in the past. However, private mediation always goes into financial and property issues. The choice is up to the spouses.

Q: Is divorce mediation right for everybody?

A: No. Successful mediation requires that both husband and wife be cooperative, willing to compromise and have a sincere interest in coming to terms over the particular issues involved. Mediation would be virtually impossible for marriages with a history of physical abuse, for instance, or for a woman or man who has been abandoned. On the other hand, many couples, whose communication has broken down, find it easier to re-establish communication with a third neutral party present.

Q: I like the idea of mediated divorce; but I'm afraid I'll end up the loser. My spouse is a much better arguer than I, and always got the last word in our arguments. Wouldn't I be better off protected by a lawyer who can do the talking for me?

A: As a matter of fact, you're just the sort of person who can benefit the most from divorce mediation. A mediator has been trained to balance the communication between you and your spouse. He or she will carefully monitor the number of interruptions and the amount of "air-time" for each spouse. In this way, mediation becomes a very effective form of protection for you. And unlike turning over your case to a lawyer, it still allows you to make your own decisions.

(A credit line, mentioning the name and address of the publishing association, corporate sponsor or both, may appear at the bottom of page 8.)

The preceding brochure copy was written to fit a 3 3/4 inches by 8 1/2 inches page, which fits into a standard number ten office envelop. This will make mailing easy, efficient and economical. The copy was written to a count of 55 characters per line with a maximum length of 51 lines per printed page. This comes to an estimated eight words per line, approximately 400 words per printed page or a total of approximately 2800 words for the entire brochure. Only seven of the eight pages are counted since the first page is the booklet's cover.

The copy can be adapted or revised in any number of ways. The important thing in creating and distributing such a printed piece is that it creates a favorable awareness of divorce mediation.

## Press Kit

Most publicity efforts are normally "pitched" or sold with the help of written materials. A press kit, consisting of a variety of press releases, fact sheets, photographs and the like, should be sent to broadcasters and editors in your city. A "pitch letter" should be sent describing the spokesperson and explaining why his or her message is important.

The ideal press kit for divorce mediation should include the following:

- A lead or feature press release on the selected message.
- A general press release on divorce mediation.
- A biography of the spokesperson.
- An black & white, 8" x 10" photograph of the spokesperson.
- A fact sheet on divorce mediation.
- A list of suggested questions and answers for the interviewer.
- A copy of the divorce mediation brochure.

Sample copy and formats for these press kit elements and for the accompanying press releases appear on the following pages. For the sake of readability, hypothetical names have been given to the spokesperson, publicist and broadcaster involved in these communications.

A professionally done press kit should be offset-printed or very clearly copied by a good copy machine on the sponsoring organization's or public relations firm's letterhead. Releases of more than one page should be stapled together. Photographs should be identified with a caption printed on letterhead or plain white paper and attached with rubber cement to the lower back of the photograph so that the paper can be folded across the face of the photo.

All releases, fact sheets and photo captions should include the name of the publicity contact and his or her phone number as well as a release date. If the news is to be released to the public only after a specific date, the date should be given at the top of each release, e.g., For Release on or after April 1,

1995. If the information can be printed or broadcasted at any time, the phrase "For Immediate Release" should be used instead.

When several releases and other materials are to be mailed or presented together as a complete press kit, they should be placed inside a folder with one or more inside pockets. The front of the folder should bear the name of the sponsoring organization and/or the name of the project itself.

The pitch letter, if any, may be attached to the front of the folder with a paper clip. In publicity, as in most marketing efforts, both style and substance play important roles.

After the press kit is written you may want to send it out in conjunction with possible events and occasions. Some tie-ins could include:

- June: Traditional month for weddings. Statisticians tell us that half of these weddings will end in divorce. "The Latest Trends in Marriage and Divorce."

- Valentine's Day: Same reverse angle as June. While many are professing their love, others are trying to end love relationships. Divorce Mediation is a less painful way of doing so.

- Father's Day: How the role of fathers is changing particularly in divorce. "Why Divorce Mediation Is Appealing to Fathers?"

- 1995: 20th Anniversary of California's no-fault divorce law (1970), which ultimately affected the way an entire country looked at divorce. "Has It Lived Up to Its Promise?"

- 1998: 35th Anniversary of the founding of the Association of Family and Conciliation Courts (1963).

- Newly-released survey reveals how Americans feel about divorce; and boy are they still mad. Selected information from the Kindred Spirits survey.

- National conference on "Divorce and Its Effects on Children."

- Local seminars on "Divorce and Its Effects on Children."

- Mediation spokesperson's local lecture engagement to a group of professionals such as attorneys & therapists.

- New study reveals trends in divorce. Discussion on what factors account for a "successful" divorce.

These are some examples of events and conferences that could be organized. The expertise and reputation of the spokesperson could also be useful for planning events.

<u>**Sample Press Release**</u>

Contact: Jane Doe
          (212)123-4567                    <u>For Immediate Release</u>

### SERIAL MONOGAMY IN THE 90'S:
### STUDY SHOWS DIVORCE DOESN'T HAVE
### TO BE A TRAUMA

"Nobody enjoys going through a divorce," says Divorce Mediator, Robert Meeker. "But some people do a lot better than others in terms of coming out stronger, happier and with a higher self-esteem."

Who are these people who have had, what some sociologists are now calling, "successful divorces?" They're the men and women who have worked out their divorce agreements through divorce mediation.

A national survey of more than 300 divorced men and women revealed a direct correlation between having gone through divorce mediation and positive post-divorce feelings. Spouses have reported satisfaction with custody and visitation arrangements, and compliance with these arrangements. They noted their own sense of competence and a greater self-esteem. And their children, the parents reported, are also more satisfied. People, who have opted for a traditional litigated divorce, had negative experiences which left them feeling angry and empty.

"One of the reasons this is true," explains Meeker, is that mediation allows both husband and wife to express their points of view in a controlled setting. The agreements reached are their own; they are not settlements made for them by attorneys or judges. When you are in control of your own life, you're more likely to be happy with your decisions.

*###*

Contact: Jane Doe
          (212) 123-4567                    <u>For Immediate Release</u>

A Guide to Divorce Mediation
Or, How to Be Civilized in
an Otherwise Uncivilized World


In the United States, when two people disagree, the tendency is to sue each other. However this litigious attitude may be changing, and a number of successful lawyers are in the forefront of the movement toward civilized dispute resolution.

Mediation is the word to remember - the process being used more often by divorcing couples. Until a decade or two ago, the United States had adopted the use of mediation in only labor-management relations. The success of mediation in this environment sets the stage for later uses - the most prominent being divorce mediation.

In divorce mediation, a couple, who have made the decision to end their marriage, retains a mediator usually on a per session basis to help them work out an agreement. The mediator may be an attorney, or a mental health professional. No matter what the background, a person has to go through special training in order to become a mediator.

The mediator and the two spouses meet together for several sessions to make important decisions about financial arrangements, property settlements, custody, visitation, etc. The mediator's goal, unlike a counselor or therapist, is not to discuss the past or try to resolve past emotional issues. The mediator focuses on the present and future "pragmatic" relations of the couple.

The mediator is, furthermore, not an arbitrator since he or she does not make the final decision for the couple, but rather helps the couple come to a mutually satisfactory agreement. The mediator is a completely neutral and objective third party, who maintains balance in the sessions.

More and more Americans are turning to divorce mediation rather than retaining separate and adversarial attorneys since it offers some very real benefits. They are happier with the agreement since it is their own, and they are more likely to stick to the arrangement especially for visitation schedules, child support payments and other custody related terms. Mediation, in general, is less expensive and saves the couple time. Others turn to mediation simply because it is a more private environment than court, particularly for discussing the kinds of emotional issues involved in many divorces.

### ###

## Sample Fact Sheet

Contact:        Jane Doe
                (212)123-4567        <u>For Immediate Release</u>


FACT SHEET: DIVORCE MEDIATION

Description:    A non-adversarial process through which a
                divorcing couple meet with a trained mediator in
                order to design their own divorce agreement.

U.S. History:   Mediation was used almost exclusively in labor
                relations until recently.

Time:           Sessions normally last 1 to 2 hours.

Sessions:       The number of sessions depends on the
                complexity of the issues.

Expenses:       Rates vary widely.  One study showed that
                couples who enter mediation end up paying lower
                fees for their divorce.

Other Benefits: - Less damage to relationship between spouses.
                - Overall satisfaction with decision, especially
                  for the parent who does not have custody of
                  the children.
                - Fewer infractions on agreement for visitation
                  and child support.
                - Lower likelihood of going to court.

Mediator Profile: Fifteen percent of mediators are attorneys, ten
                percent are psychologists, twenty-two percent
                are psychiatrists and 40 percent are social
                workers.  Eight out of ten hold graduate
                degrees.

## Sample Question and Answer Sheet

Contact: Jane Doe
     (212)123-4567          For Immediate Release

Suggested Questions and Answers for
Robert Meeker, Divorce Mediator

Q: What exactly is divorce mediation, and why should people bother to learn about it?

A: First of all, people should care because the odds are very high that they will be effected directly or indirectly by divorce. We're living in a world now where divorce is the norm.

     It's time that we take divorce out of the courtroom, a place where criminals are tried for crimes, and into a civilized and private environment. This allows for the possibility of maintaining a friendly relationship between the couple and a positive parenting relationship with the children.

Q: How is mediation better for the children?

A: I think we - the adults in America - are laboring under the major misconception, a really outdated point of view, that children of divorce go through terrible traumas and are scarred for life. The fact is that your child may handle the experience better than you. After all, at least half of the kids, whom he or she goes to school with and plays with, come from what we used to call "broken homes." Today's generation of children are amazingly at home with the idea of step-families, ex-husbands and wives, and joint custody.

     What traumatizes children is not the fact of divorce. It's the anger, the fury, the revenge that becomes a part of their parents' attitudes toward each other after their marriage is over.

And divorce mediation can go a long way toward minimizing that kind of negative impact.

Q: But is it a practical way to divorce?  Don't you need a divorce lawyer at some point?

A: First of all, everyone should know that many divorce mediators are lawyers themselves.  A considerable number of divorce lawyers have started practicing mediation because they've seen the emotional damage that is caused by litigation. In fact, the modern, divorce mediation movement was founded by a divorce lawyer - the late O.J. Coogler, who had a difficult divorce and was determined to find a better way.  And that he did.

　　　If the mediator, with whom you choose to work, is not an attorney, then he or she may work with one as part of a team or may be part of a law firm.  Or, the mediator may ask you to use your own family lawyer after the final agreement is written. Really all that needs to be done is to have the final agreement, the decision that you have made, reviewed and approved by an attorney in the end.

Q: If a couple is rational and willing to cooperate can't they just sit down at the kitchen table and negotiate between themselves? Do they really need a mediator?

A: This type of couple is very rare and I doff my hat to them. For most of us, though, going through a divorce is emotionally turbulent.  This is why you need an objective, clear-headed professional to monitor the proceedings, to guide you through the issues that you've decided to have mediated.

　　　The two of you may need some help in fighting fair and in allowing equal "air-time."  A good mediator can work wonders for a spouse who has never gotten the last word in an argument during all the years of marriage.

Q: How long has divorce mediation been around?  It sounds great; but it makes me wonder why one doesn't hear more about it.

A: In the grand scheme of history, divorce mediation hasn't been around long.  However, in its almost 40 years of history, it has become an important profession with dozens of books and magazine articles written about it.  There exist professional associations such as the Academy of Family Mediators, and professional journals devoted completely to family mediation.

But one of the reasons why I think mediation is not better known is because of the old saying: "No news is good news."  The peaceful settlements that come out of mediation are not high drama.  So, you don't hear about them.  You only read or hear about the divorce cases in court that are vicious - cases where famous people call spouses names and do incredibly hostile things.  In fact, I'm glad that mediated divorces don't make the front pages.  Honestly they don't belong there anyway.

They have a name for the kinds of divorce lawyers who are out for blood.  They are called "bombers."  And frankly, their stories make better copy than a story about two rational, sensible, civilized people sitting down and working things out.

Q: There seems to be a lot of vicious divorces in the news.  Is this really that bad?  Maybe it's good for the couples to work out their hostilities.  In any case, if a marriage is over, it's over.

A: I'll tell you why I disagree with this idea.  A marriage may be over, but the relationship never is, especially when children are involved.  A family is forever.

You can walk out the door of your home tomorrow morning and never walk back in again.  You can say you're through with your spouse.  But that marriage always will be a part of you.  You are still the mother or father of your children.  So, the two of you will always have ties.

A court is a fine place for two people who want to battle it out and never see each other again, or for, perhaps, a corporation and a consumer. But it's a terrible place for two people who once loved each other and may have children. A mediator's private office is a much more conducive place to work issues out. The goal is to be the best possible ex-husband and ex-wife since this is part of your responsibility for being a good parent.

Q: How does one go about finding a divorce mediator?

A: The same way you go about finding any professional - doctor, lawyer, accountant, therapist. You may ask your family lawyer if he or she practices mediation. The American Bar Association established standards and practices for mediation.

Since mediation isn't as established yet as other professions, you may not have as much luck asking friends and associates for recommendations. But you can ask other professionals to recommend someone such as your lawyer, therapist, marriage counselor, even your minister. The Academy of Family Mediators has standards for their members and can guide you to someone who practices in your area.

###

## Sample Pitch Letter

April 1, 1995


Mr. Robert Bastanhury, Talent Coordinator
A.M. Los Angeles
KABC-TV
4151 Prospect Avenue
Hollywood, CA 90028

Dear Mr. Bastanhury:

It's time to stop bemoaning America's once astonishing divorce rates, and accept divorce as a fact of life. In fact, according to the advocates of divorce mediation, it's time to make divorce the rational and civilized process that it should be.

The idea of "successful divorce" or of becoming a good ex-spouse may seem outlandish, but guidance in these areas is available and much needed in the 1990s.

Robert Meeker, a divorce mediator, is an expert on the subject. He has a lot of valuable information to pass along to your thousands of viewers who are thinking about divorce.

A press kit with information on Mr. Meeker and the mediation process is enclosed. I'll call you next week in hopes that we can set up an interview for him on A.M. Los Angeles. Thank you for your interest.

Sincerely,

Jane Doe
Media Specialist


enc.

It should be noted that all of the preceding sample press kit materials have been presented in as realistic a format as possible within this paper. Fact sheets are customarily printed single-spaced, and press releases and the like are generally double-spaced.

The study described in the first press release is purely imaginary, although it is certainly plausible that such a study will yield such results.

A photograph should be included, when the real spokesperson has been found. It is important to include this photo since many press people, particularly those in television want to know what any prospective interviewee looks like, before making a final decision about booking him or her. The inclusion of a spokesperson photo is standard operating procedure.

When preparing for broadcast interviews, the spokesperson should be familiar with the particularly difficult questions that might be asked. A list like the one that follows should be completely rehearsed before any media appearance.

Q1: Isn't it true that a lot of divorce mediators are poorly qualified. In fact, can't anyone call him or herself a divorce mediator and go into practice tomorrow?

A1: I'm happy to say that all that is changing rapidly. I think, five years from now, you'll find the practice of mediation licensed and controlled just the way law and medicine are. The American Bar Association has set standards for practice. And the Academy of Family mediators is very much involved in this issue. A lot is going on to standardize the profession now.

But of course, if you're getting divorced right now, what's going to happen five years from now doesn't do you much good. What you need to do, when choosing a divorce mediator at this time, is to ask for the person's background and ask them for their credentials and qualifications. A good credential would be someone who has studied with O.J. Coogler or received training from John Haynes. Also, the Academy of

Family Mediators has a list of training programs that are acceptable for membership in their organization.

Remember that just because a person has a law degree or a psychiatry or psychology degree does not mean that he or she is a trained mediator. These credentials are impressive and probably helpful for mediation, but you want to work with someone who has been trained in mediation, who knows the art of mediation backwards, forewords and upside down. Someone well-trained will make a difference in how your divorce turns out and how satisfied you will be with the outcome in the near and far future.

Q2: Won't mediation be doubly expensive since you eventually have to work with a lawyer?

A2: It sounds that way, doesn't it? But in practice, it doesn't turn out that way at all. You are more likely to work things out faster in mediation than you would in a litigated case.

People, who go to a mediator, then who go to a lawyer to review the agreement, end up spending less because all the work has been done already for the lawyer. In a study done by the Divorce Mediation Research Project in the early 1980s, almost half the people who went through litigated divorce spent quite a bit more than their counterparts going through mediation. Even the people, who started in mediation and didn't finish, ended up spending less.

So, even if you think that a traditional litigated divorce is the right method for you, you may want to give mediation a shot for one or two sessions. You may prefer it, and it may save you money, time and - don't forget - mental anguish.

Q3: The way it sounds; divorce mediation is a great idea for people who get along, trust each other, can communicate well and are willing to compromise. The trouble is people like that don't get divorced. Isn't the idea pretty useless when one spouse thinks the other is irrational?

A3: The beauty of divorce mediation is that, if done well, it enables people with real communication problems to get past some of them. The presence of the objective, third party and his or her skills makes the difference.

I'm not saying that mediation is fun or easy. But I am saying that you're going to see a lot less tension, anger, and impediments than you would in court or in an adversarial lawyer's office.

Pretty much divorce mediation is for everyone. I'll tell you for whom divorce mediation is not. It's not for a spouse who has been physically abused, or for a spouse with serious substance abuse problems. And it can't help abandoned spouses.

Q4: The thing that worries me about divorce mediation, as you describe it, is that it just doesn't sound like smart business. A lot of people want to get the best possible arrangement from the divorce. Doesn't divorce mediation require two people who are not concerned about their own benefits?

A4: In Japan, mediation has a very important role in dispute resolution, both in personal and professional life. Yet the Japanese are successful business people. Everyone is writing books about the Japanese Superpower. The point is that if it can work for them, it can work for us. By trying to maintain a balance in the couple's future life, one may find that it is actually better business, and the arrangements may be more acceptable for both than the one decided in a divorce court.

Q5: I knew a woman who went to a divorce mediator for a couple sessions with her husband, and then, out of the blue, she received a call from his attorney. Behind her back, he had hired a "bomber" divorce lawyer, instead of finishing mediation. She was forced to hire one in retaliation. How can mediation protect against such an outcome?

A5: What happened to this woman is not the norm. The vast majority of people, who enter mediation, stay with it. And the vast majority, who come to an agreement, are both equally satisfied with it.

It's important to remember that, like all professions, some mediators' skills are better than others. My guess is that this particular mediator had not done his or her job well. It may be that the husband hadn't been helped to feel as empowered, as competent, as much a part of the decision-making process, as he should have been. Otherwise, he would not have needed to have made this sneaky maneuver. This is why it is important to find a mediator that you both feel confident about; so, that you will both see things to the end.

Q6: The bottom line is that people feel safer when they have the protection of the courts and the legal system. Can divorce mediation give this to people?

A6: The real disappointment lies in wait for the person who really believes this. A lot of people really believe that judges are descendants of King Solomon - that they will be saved by the wisdom of the judge. The fact is that a judge's wisdom can only be applied when there is a question of right and wrong. In most divorce cases, no one is in the right and no one is in the wrong. It is just a matter of two people whose values are no longer compatible. Leaving someone so intimate makes one feel very insecure, and it is natural that both spouses will not feel very safe. Trying to come to a divorce agreement in a litigious environment only aggravates this sense of insecurity and loss of safety. On the hand, a peaceful environment will only foster a better agreement and make both spouses feel secure about the decision and the future.

In addition to specific events and campaign-specific advertising efforts like the public service print and broadcast ads, effective public relations must include on-going efforts to place feature articles in the media. This is a labor intensive process, but if the following game plan is followed, then the effort will be successful.

Editors and broadcasters must be contacted by telephone and/or in person about specific articles or segment ideas. It is best to try to establish a good relationship with these people. Arrange personal interviews between the editor or broadcaster and the spokesperson. Generally many editors and broadcasters have to be approached in order to find the "perfect" match. Don't despair and be persistent.

The objective of public relations is to give credibility and acceptance to divorce mediation. One article in a national, popular journal or magazine, such as "People," or one appearance on a major talk show, such as "Oprah," can be more helpful in furthering your efforts than a dozen, smaller public relations efforts. However, such placements are the most difficult to obtain, and, generally, come after the dozen, smaller ones. Good timing does play a part as well when educating the more important editors or producers. However don't neglect that newsworthiness and persistence are equally important factors.

You may have more luck giving one editor an "exclusive" over the phone, in person or in writing, or all three. Generally is it a good idea to send an "exclusive" press release no matter what. On the following pages are examples of such releases. Some of the information in these sample releases are hypothetical. For the campaign, actual cases, anecdotes and studies should be found and should replace those presented here.

## Sample Feature Release #1

Contact: Jane Doe                    For Immediate Release
(212)123-4567                        Exclusive to Vanity Fair


The New Hollywood Divorce:
Tinseltown Teaches America
About Serial Monogamy - Again

By Kathy McIntosh


When I was growing up in Wisconsin and reading fan magazines by the gross, I used to amaze friends by being able to name Elizabeth Taylor's husbands - in order. Her full name, I would recite, was Elizabeth Rosemond Taylor Hilton Wilding Todd Fisher Burton. (A Burton reprise and a Warner were added later, but by then I no longer read fan magazines openly.)

It was all pretty shocking to a generation of Midwesterners growing up in the 1950s and early 1960s. There had never been a divorce in our family, and only one or two in our community. Only in that far-off land, called Hollywood, did seemingly sane adults change marriage partners on much the same schedule as my father traded cars.

It was fascinating, but utterly foreign. Through Hollywood, I became familiar with such alien concepts as custody battles, property settlements and alimony. From fan magazines, I learned to use terms like "her ex-" and "his child from a previous marriage." Hollywood taught us all how to think about divorce.

I don't live in Wisconsin anymore, but I stay in touch with those who remained. It's incredible; since the late 1980s, at least half of my cousins have "ex's," and they are still welcomed at family reunions. Most of the people, with whom I went to high school, have been divorced at least once, like myself. In fact, a few of the women have almost as many last names as Elizabeth Taylor. When I hear about custody battles now, it's more likely to be an anecdote about an old college friend's marital woes, not about a movie star's.

In fact, it seemed that the trend to divorce in Hollywood had become passe and became part of a public trend. I just didn't hear anymore stories about this star's disastrous divorce, and that one's near bankruptcy divorce story. Yet married stars were not staying together in matrimonial bliss. They were getting divorces.

I discovered that the stars were now concerned about the how the publicity and name-calling was effecting their children. And thus, they were having quiet divorces out of the courts and out of the reach of the gossip journalists. They were trying to settle their divorces through mediation.

"I've tried divorce both ways," explains Heather Youngblood, star of ABC-TV's award winning "Age Before Beauty," "and definitely there is no comparison to mediation's civilized style.

"I got my first divorce, when I was twenty-five and our child was four. I had my first taste of success; it was the year that Highrise (her first film) came out. And I really believed that to be a star, I had to cut my husband up in court.

"I hired a bomber lawyer because I could afford to do so. I won -- if you can call it that. But it was the most awful six months of my life. Going on both our lawyers' advice, we ripped each other to shreds in court.

"It's been ten years since, and I'm still furious when I think about some of the things he said about me in public. I'm sure he feels the same way about me. But the saddest thing of all is that he hasn't seen our daughter since she was six. He wasn't happy with the visitation schedule set up by the court. As the months passed, he became more and more angry, until he couldn't come see her anymore.

"I gave up a lot to get my divorce the 'right' way."

When Youngblood separated from agent-producer, Martin Swindell earlier this year, she remembered the pain and unhappiness of her first divorce, and suggested that they visit

Beverly Hills based mediator Anna Kramer.  Kramer, whose hourly fees top those of many distinguished attorneys, had mediated the divorces of Bill and Connie Sumners, Sally Hoffman and Rob Cruise, Maria Tompkins and Arnold Rivera, and others.

Mediation, a private and peaceful process, is about as un-Hollywood as you can imagine.  Two people, who want a divorce, sit together in a private office, where they quietly negotiate the terms of their divorce.  They will determine: who gets custody of the children, visitation schedules, who gets the house, and decide on how to split joint investments and other financial arrangements.

When the two have come to an agreement on all matters that concern them, then an attorney will draw up a legal document, which will be signed by them both.  No pre-trial publicity.  No star entrances at court.  No accusations of infidelity, mental cruelty or irreconcilable differences.

"I think divorce has finally matured," says Anna Kramer, a slim woman of forty-five years, whose charcoal gray suit and slight British accent might seem more at home on Bond Street than Rodeo Drive.

###

**Sample Feature Release #2**

Contact: Jane Doe                    For Immediate Release
         (212) 123-4567              Exclusive to People


Don Payne Turns Divorce Upside Down:
He Leaves Them Smiling All Across America


In New York these days, a Don Payne divorce is almost as chic as a Park Avenue address or a Ralph Lauren suit. And Payne is not a divorce lawyer who guarantees to get you all the money from the joint bank accounts. In fact, he does practically the opposite.

He's not an attorney. He's not a psychiatrist. He's not a marriage counselor. He's -- well, what is he anyway? He is a divorce mediator, a term coined by the late O.J. Coogler, who is Payne's only competitor for the title of "Father of Divorce Mediation." Coogler, who was a Georgian lawyer, went through a divorce of his own, and, still dazed by the emotional blows, was determined to find a better solution to end a marriage. What he started in 1978 has grown into a full-fledged phenomenon - divorce mediators all over North America, court-mandated mediation in several states, and licensing on the horizon for attorneys, therapists, and other professionals who practice it.

There are hundreds, maybe thousands of mediators, calmly helping unhappy couples negotiate their custody, visitation and financial agreements. Payne, however, is the field's first star. Mediators say that the experience of watching Payne talk a couple through a difficult, sticky issue is like watching Picasso at his canvas. He makes it look easy, but no one else can duplicate his results. Perhaps, this is why he has to turn down four out of five requests for him to handle a case.

Mediation is an art," explains Payne, a lean 6'3" New Englander who looks more like a professor than an expert on matrimonial woes. "You never know who will be naturally talented at it. I've seen brilliant trial lawyers who couldn't mediate their way out of a paper bag. And I've seen others, men and women, whose law careers were anything but fast-track, but could facilitate communication on their first try like practiced professionals.

Payne is not a lawyer himself, although a sizeable percentage of mediators are former or present jurists. A native of Arlington, Massachusetts, he began his career in labor relations where he made a strong impression on both management and union leaders. He wanted a career change and started to study sociology. He heard whispers of divorce mediation, which was just beginning to catch on. He knew immediately that he had found his niche.

It's an unusual career choice for a man who's been happily married since 1964. He and wife, Mara, live in New York's suburban Westchester County with two of their three daughters, Allison, 18 and Shannon, 15. Their eldest, Jennifer, 25, is a recent law school graduate living in Washington, DC. Despite this Norman Rockwell picture of idyllic family life, Payne considers, the acceptance of divorce by the public as a fact of life, his *raison d'etre*. "I'm not anti-family by any means. On the contrary, if you have children, then there will always be a family. If you have loved and lived with another person, their influence on your life will remain with you always. Divorce just changes the shapes of things."

The doctrine, he preaches, is often referred to as "successful divorce." In imparting his professional philosophy, he teaches the soon-to-be divorced how to be good ex-spouses to each other. He stresses that not knowing how to be a good ex-husband or ex-wife will effect your ability to be a good single parent. "Just because people can't live together as husband and wife does not mean they can't get along under other circumstances," he stated to a conference of aspiring mediators last month. "In fact, it doesn't mean they can't get along better than ever. Being a good ex-spouse hasn't been on the top of people's priority lists; but that's only because the concept hasn't been around for long. Now people get divorced because their life goals aren't the same or one spouse has to find him or herself. Divorce has a completely different sociological role in current society."

Payne adds with a wink that people will look back on this society generations from now, and laugh at the way we handled divorce in the 20th century. "I can hear them regaling each other with tales about the old days. They'll tell each other stories of divorces held in court as though divorcing couples were criminals like murderers, thieves ... 'And sometimes, they made their children testify against each other. Wasn't it barbaric back then?'"

Some observers believe the growing trend toward mediation is a return to traditional values of civility and privacy updated for a world in which multiple marriages are commonplace. Advocates point out the many advantages of mediation over litigated adversarial divorce. It generally saves time and money. The parent, who doesn't get custody, is more likely to be happy with the visitation and child support arrangements, and, therefore, will be more likely to abide by them. It also tends to reduce hostilities, rather than increase them (some divorce lawyers are accused of encouraging this). And it actually can improve the relationship between the two spouses, rather than leading to further conflict, as litigated divorces often do.

The most important benefit, though, is mediation's impact on self-esteem. "Handing control of your divorce over to adversarial lawyers may feel like a relief, but it also renders you powerless in many ways. Successfully getting through mediation does just the opposite. The men and women, who go through it, emerge with a real sense of accomplishment and competence. And there's never a time in your life, when you're going to need to feel like this more."

###

**Sample Feature Release #3**

Contact: Jane Doe                    For Immediate Release
(212)123-4567                         Exclusive to Redbook


Seven (Reasonably) Easy Ways to Become
the Best Ex-Wife on Your Block


Sociologists call it the "multiple role phenomenon" because it's the multiple roles that women have to play in today's society: wife, mother, businesswoman, dutiful daughter, lover, friend, general angel of mercy. Choose any combination of the above and you have the multiple role phenomenon. All these roles, keep her busy, or may leave her confused. Studies have shown, however, that it may actually make her happy. The woman with several sources of fulfillment is more likely to describe herself as satisfied with her life overall.

One role, though, is relatively new. It's possible that your grandmother never met one - or, if she had, she wouldn't have entertained her in the front parlor. She's the ex-wife; and there's a 50-50 chance that you may become one.

Not so many decades ago, when divorce was a relatively uncommon occurrence, the best one could say about ex-wives was "Don't become one." Now people are saying "Try to be a good ex-wife." Colin Bradlee, author of "Real Life Etiquette" (1987) remembers the only rule of etiquette for ex-spouses was "where to seat the divorced mother and father of the bride or groom, and how to word the wedding invitation in such a situation."

Marilyn Cater, psychology professor of University of Maryland, has published several studies on post-divorce relationships. She remarked that "the assumption used to be that once two people were divorced, it didn't matter how they behaved, or that they had societal permission to behave badly.

This sort of behavior has done a lot of damage to the men, women and children involved."

The basic misunderstanding, many experts agree, is that people believed a divorce ended the family, or, at least, the relationship between the husband and wife. Yet, in most cases, these relationships continue, as originally planned, 'til death do them part. Joe DiMaggio, although ex-husband to Marilyn Monroe, still placed roses on her grave every year. His gesture reflected the on-going connection between two people who have loved, married, and divorced.

Attorney and divorce mediator, _____, believes that the goal of any divorcing couple should be to have a "successful" divorce. He suggests following these guidelines:

1. Shed your old skin:
Before you can become a good ex-wife, you have to make the distinction between the old role and the new. As an ex-wife, you have a right to feel jealous of his new wife or girlfriend, but you don't have the right to act on it. You have a right to his help with the children, but not with the downstairs plumbing. You have a right to be treated with respect, but not to be put first on his priority list. Consider your ex-husband to be a good friend to whom you owe certain loyalties, but with whom you'd never want to live. (You can probably think of a lot of people who'd fall into this category.)

2. Divide your life into periods:
If artists can have blue periods or cubists periods, then it stands to reason that most other human beings go through distinct and separate eras in their emotional lives. It's helpful actually to take out a piece of paper and draw a line representing a projected eighty years of life, then divide it into sections. Label them childhood, high school, college, the names of cities you've lived in, companies you've worked for, and the men that you've dated, and the man that you married. Now look at all the fresh space ahead. You can look back on your David, Stephen, Tom

period for the rest of your life, but it clearly exists apart from either the present or the future.

## 3. Consider divorce mediation:

If ex-wife is a new role, into which you will enter, there may still be time to reach your separation and divorce agreements through mediation, rather than through an adversarial process. Numerous studies have shown that husband-wife relationships suffer less damage when things are worked out with the help of a mediator, rather than through litigation, adversarial lawyers and court. Even if you've been divorced for a while, seeing a mediator might be helpful. He or she could help the two of you work out any arrangements that are giving you problems (e.g., visitation schedules, financial details). Some lawyers and mental health professionals are trained mediators, or can help you find one.

## 4. Keep your promises:

Living up to the agreement, which you've made with your ex-spouse, is an important part of being a good ex-wife. Research has shown that couples who have had their divorces mediated are far more likely than others to respect their divorce agreements. Mostly this is due to the fact that they were directly involved in designing the agreement, rather than having it dictated to them.

## 5. Always respect him in front of your children:

It's tempting to complain about your ex-husband's failings to your most available audience - the children. But this can do damage all around. At the very least, they'll wonder why you chose to marry a man whom you regard negatively. Remember his good qualities (even if you think they've mysteriously disappeared) and mention them when you can.

## 6. Remember the good times:

No matter how awful life with your ex-husband has become or how painful the process of separation and divorce was, there were some happy moments during the marriage. Share these stories with your children, just as you would any family anecdote. It's important for them to know about the good times of the marriage -- and it's important for you to remember.

7. Accept the divorce:
The only danger in remembering your ex-husband and former marriage so fondly is that reconciliation can begin to look all too appealing. This happens in fairy tales and sometimes, but very rarely, in real life. However, the odds are against it. Being an exemplary ex-wife is part of being a good parent and a good person, but it's only one of the many roles in your future. Developing the other sides of your life will help keep things in perspective.

###

## Seminars

A seminar or conference on divorce mediation, by bringing together experts from different fields in order to discuss various issues related to America's high divorce rate, can be an effective, public relations, media event. It should be promoted as a gathering of legal, mental health, and academic professionals whose work brings them into constant contact with contemporary divorce and its effects.

A one-day conference could be held in a city hotel or conference center, with invitations going to interested attorneys, psychiatrists, psychologists, social workers, marriage and family counselors, clergy, and university professors in these fields. Invitations should also be issued in advance to media representatives from television and radio news programs, consumer magazines (women's, men's and general interest pages of the daily newspaper), weekly and daily newspapers, and news wire services.

The program could consist of individual presentations and panel discussions on approximately half a dozen different divorce-related topics. Suggested topics are as follows:

- **I Know One Child Whose Parents Are Still Married**
  Children and Divorce: Social Development Concern in an Era when the Broken Family Is the Norm.

- **Let's Behave Like Rational Adults**
  The Future of Divorce Mediation in the 90s.

- **Children on the City-Suburb Shuttle**
  New Directions in Joint Custody Arrangements.

- **Divorce, Japanese or Chinese Style?**
  Eastern vs. Western Thought in Conflict Resolution.

- **It's Only Their First Marriage**
  Serial Monogamy as a Planned Lifestyle.

## - Pre-Nuptial Agreements: The First Decade
Their Consumers, Contents, and Effects on Separation.
and Divorce Agreements

Research on the benefits of divorce mediation can be worked legitimately into several of the presentations. You or your organization's name should appear on the event's program, on a sign behind the speaker's platform (so that it will be seen, at least partially, in news photographs) and on all publicity materials distributed to representatives of the media.

A final press kit should be mailed to broadcast and print media, summarizing the presentations. The result should bring about considerable local media coverage, particularly in daily newspapers and local television-news programs.

# CHAPTER 5

## Public Relations Plan for the
## Individual Mediator or Mediation Service

When an earthquake claims hundreds of lives in South America or Asia, the Kansas City TV stations look for a seismologist in Kansas City. When a major political news story comes out of the Soviet Union, the newspaper reporters in New Orleans look for a professor of Russian Studies or Political Science at Tulane. "What does it mean?" they ask. "What should our viewers, listeners or readers know about it? What do you think?" The need for and customary use of local experts in news and feature stories of all kinds can be the key to successful local promotion.

The challenge for the individual divorce mediator is to educate the media about the concept of divorce mediation. For this goal, the individual mediator may use concepts and materials previously outlined in this book. Press releases, booklets, and background materials on mediation can be effective in explaining this relatively unknown (or misunderstood) process to local media people.

A more personalized approach should be adopted. Although it may be distasteful at first to many mediators, professional people must be introduced to the public in much the same ways that other well-known people from soap opera stars to senators have been. This is to say that the techniques are identical; the messages, fortunately, are not.

Before one can build oneself visibly within the public, one must establish some visibility with the press. Even in smaller cities, the staffs of television stations, radio stations and newspapers act as gatekeepers through whom the vast majority of our information about the world must pass.

In other words, before John and Julie Smith can know that Paul Higgins is an experienced and expert mediator in their city, anchorwoman Heidi Thomas has to be told and given reason to believe it. Only when Higgins is interviewed on the local evening news or for the local newspaper do the Smiths become aware of his existence. Only then can they give thought to consulting him for their own impending divorce.

## Press Kit

A press kit for an individual mediator should contain the following items:
- A general release on divorce mediation (including quotes from the mediator).
- An individual biography of the mediator.
- A captioned photograph of him or her.

When a media representative asks for material on an individual, these are the basic items that should be sent. Other items, which may be included in the press kit, are:
- Feature releases on specific aspects of divorce mediation.
- Magazine and/or newspaper clippings about divorce mediation.
- Magazine and/or newspaper clippings about the mediator.
- Booklets or pamphlets on mediation services.

    - Suggested interview questions and answers on the
      subject of divorce mediation.

Clippings are particularly valuable in building credibility. At the beginning of a public relations program, it is unlikely that a mediator will have clippings in which he or she has been interviewed. At that point, however, clippings about mediation in general can be inserted. They give the reporter, editor or broadcaster some background information about the process and prove that other media people have taken mediation seriously enough to write about it.

      Clippings should be selected on the basis of the prestige and/or recognizability of the publication in which the article appeared, and on the length and favorable tone of the article itself. That is, even a four-line mention of divorce mediation or a local practitioner can be impressive if it appeared in "Time," "Newsweek," "The Wall Street Journal," or "The Washington Post." On the other hand, a clipping from an obscure magazine or a small weekly newspaper can have considerable impact if it is particularly well-written, dramatic in presentation, very favorable for the subject or all three.

      It is not necessary to obtain original copies of the articles or to order glossy tear sheets of them. Even large public relations firms duplicate articles on the office copy machine and insert those copies into press kits.

      On the following pages are samples of press releases and bios that might be used by an individual mediator seeking local, regional or even national coverage.

## Sample General Press Release for Individual Mediators

For Immediate Release:
Contact: (612)765-4321


Divorce in the 21st Century Will Be
"A Whole New Ball Game"


When people in the nineteenth century tried to imagine life in the future, they may have envisioned manned air flight, spaceships, and fabulous new time-saving inventions. It's doubtful, however, that any of them predicted the change in our attitudes about marriage and divorce. Queen Victoria, for one, would have been horrified.

"Maybe that's why we're botching it up so badly," suggests Minneapolis attorney and divorce mediator Katherine Reidy. "We're just new at it. As Americans (and the rest of the world) adjust to divorce and serial monogamy as a way of life, it will develop into a smoother process that is more efficient and less emotionally painful."

The first dramatic change in attitudes toward marriage, believes the 37 year old Minnesota native, is the prevalence of pre-nuptial agreements. "There's simply no reason for a couple in love to think about drawing up a pre-nuptial agreement, except that they believe the odds are against their staying married forever," she points out.

The pre-nuptial agreement is, perhaps, the first step toward correct divorce etiquette. The second step would be deciding in a civilized manner on a mutually favorable divorce agreement by meeting with a divorce mediator. In divorce mediation, the separating husband and wife meet in private sessions with a trained mediator in order to discuss and agree on custody, visitation, and financial terms.

Unlike an arbitrator, the mediator cannot dictate a decision. And unlike a traditional adversarial attorney, he or she does not act as an advocate for one spouse or the other. The mediator's job is to monitor and facilitate communication between the two spouses, assuring that neither side bullies the other nor monopolizes the discussion.

"No divorce is easy," stresses Katherine Reidy, "but some of them are successful. A number of studies have already shown that mediated divorces produce happier ex-spouses and agreements, which both parties are more likely to abide by. After all, they created the agreement themselves."

###

## Sample bio for individual mediator

For Immediate Release
Contact: (612)765-4321


Katherine Reidy
Minneapolis Attorney, Divorce Mediator and Author


Growing up in Glencoe, Minnesota (population 4,000), Katherine Reidy decided to become a lawyer while watching "Perry Mason" on TV. Twenty years later, she decided to become a divorce mediator while watching clients at her St. Paul law firm battle it out in real life.

"It's not that I hadn't developed the proper hardened sensibilities of an attorney," insists the thirty-seven year old mother of two. "I had no problem pitting two ex-business partners against each other, or two neighbors in a civil suit. But when I began to handle my first divorce cases, I knew something was wrong. These people were going to see each other again. They were divorcing, but they were still going to raise their children together. And I thought it was just plain destructive to pit them against each other in mortal battle."

Reidy, who had practiced law with some of the most prestigious firms in the area (including a five year stint with Harding, Culver, Hayden & Styles), went back to graduate school for additional course work in social work. Then, she trained with internationally known mediator John Haynes in New York.

Today, her private law practice in Minneapolis consists exclusively of divorce mediation cases. "Certainly I still practice law," she responds to those who question her career change. "It's just a different type of law that I was taught by "winner takes all" law professors." Reidy is one of the many U.S. attorneys making this decision.

Reidy has also written her first book, "Where Is Home Now?," scheduled to be published by Crown Publisher next fall. The book is a guide to life after divorce for children.

Katherine Reidy holds both a Bachelor of Arts in Political Science and a Master of Arts in Social Psychology from University of Minnesota. She received her law degree from Georgetown University. She lives in Minneapolis with her husband, David Lollar, who is an architect, and their two sons.

### ###

In her press kit, Katherine Reidy would include a photograph of herself. It should be a black and white, 5" x 7" or 8" x 10" portrait done by a professional photographer or a more informal head and shoulders shot. Photographs in press kits must always be captioned with the person's name and place of business. Although only black and white photos are necessary for the press kit, mediators should have 35 mm color slides of themselves on file in case a publication requests one. Color prints cannot be used for magazine reproduction.

Hypothetical mediator Katherine Reidy's background is standard, except for the soon-to-be published book. She should add a mention of her broadcast and print credits to her bio, as time goes on. Her bio may later read as follows:

> Reidy's more than two dozen television appearances have included segments on Eyewitness News, Noontime and Good Morning Minneapolis. Her advice has appeared in a number of local and national publications, including New Woman, Midwest Magazine, and the Minneapolis Tribune.

Other additions to a mediator's bio might include memberships in professional associations, awards and publications in which she has published articles or studies.

The most carefully written and developed press kit will be of little, real benefit, if its distribution is not handled properly. In large cities, lists of local media contacts are compiled professionally and sold to publicity-seekers in all fields. In smaller cities, mediators may have to develop their own mailing lists. This is not a serious disadvantage since even the best lists are often out of date by the time they are in print.

To create a publicity mailing list, the simplest method is the best. Have a secretary or other staff member telephone the local newspapers, magazines, television stations and radio stations, and ask to whom should materials about divorce, legal, and lifestyle issues be sent.

There may be several people for whom news about divorce mediation may be relevant at a newspaper. For one issue the business editor may be interested, or the lifestyle editor may be preparing a special issue on a related subject. On some occasions, the city desk, which handles the local news and features, might be looking for an expert on divorce or a related issue. If this is the case, all three department editors (or specific report, if those names are given out) should be put on the mailing list. At TV and radio stations, the names of program producers are generally more important than those of the hosts or anchors, names that every casual viewer knows.

Just as no resume ever should be sent out without an individually written and signed cover letter, no press kit should be mailed or messengered to a media person without a letter. Even if it is as short as "Dear Mr. Conklin: Thought you might be interested in the attached information. Best wishes, Robert Smith." The inclusion of a letter makes a positive difference.

## Public Speaking

The lecture circuit can be a highly lucrative professional sideline, but a certain amount of established celebrity is often necessary before one can command high lecture fees. The divorce mediator, who is actively marketing his or her practice should look at lectures and other public speaking engagements as opportunities for visibility, rather than profit, at least in the early years of one's marketing campaign.

In order to promote oneself as a lecturer, the first step is to establish one or more topics and outline basic speeches for each. Recommended topics for the mediator are:
- How Divorce Is Changing the Family
  (And What We Can Do about It)
- Building a New Life after Divorce
- What Single Parents Are Doing Right
- Making Peace with the Past
  (Or: How to Get Along with Your Ex-spouse, Your Spouse's Ex-spouse, Your Stepchildren, Your step-parent, etc.)

Once you have done your research, written your outline and established at least one topic on which you can speak authoritatively, the preliminary, public relations job can begin. If there are lecture bureaus in your city, you can make them aware of your availability. Although they may not be prepared to take on a new client without a well-known name or a great deal of past speaking experience, it's a good idea to make them aware of your existence. They may know organizations looking for speakers who are willing to appear for a very low fee or merely for the exposure.

Whenever possible, identify yourself in written materials as a lecturer in addition to a mediator and whatever other descriptions apply (attorney, psychologist, author, etc.). This encourages readers to see you in the speaker's role and to think of you when the need for a speaker arises.

Your biography, photograph and press release may be sent directly to presidents or program chairpeople of local clubs, schools and other organizations that are likely to hire speakers. A short note indicating your availability as a lecturer should be attached.

If you are offered lucrative lecture fees, take them by all means. If not, however, it can be a smart move, at least in the beginning, to speak to groups for free. At the most, ask for a small honorarium ($50 - $100). You might even donate that to a chosen charity. Another possibility is to ask for money or your local travel expenses only. The exposure is likely to be well worth it.

Any public speaking exposure is valuable. Its value is multiplied, however, if you are an entertaining speaker as well as an informative one. If you are not a skilled speaker you may want to look into speech classes at local colleges or adult, education organizations. If you are in a large city, look into firms that specialize in teaching executives and broadcasters to become effective communicators. The best speech coaches will videotape your performances and play them back for review and improvement. At the very least, everyone should read a guide

book on effective public speaking.   Any large bookstore will
have such books in stock, or you can order them.

Speaking engagements are likely to build a mediator's
practice both directly and indirectly.  The indirect methods are
general visibility and the possibility of media coverage of these
engagements.   More directly, some members of the audience
may well become clients as a result of having seen and heard the
speech.

## Seminars

Educational seminars open to both the public and the
media can be a dramatic means of gaining widespread visibility.
The individual mediator can choose a divorce-related topic,
which is likely to be of interest to as general an audience as
possible, and sponsor a free seminar on it.

Considerable flexibility is possible when planning and
organizing a seminar.   The following hypothetical program can
serve as a guideline.

| | |
|---|---|
| Topic: | Single Parenting 101 |
| | Redesigning the Family in the Age of Divorce |
| Sponsor: | Karasek Associates, Inc. |
| Date: | Wednesday, October 5, 1995 |
| Time: | 12:00pm - 2:00pm |
| Place: | Prudential Building |
| | 8405 Connecticut Avenue |
| | Suite 2700 |
| Speakers: | Arthur H. Karsek, Divorce Mediator |
| | Evelyn Fiori, Psychologist |
| | Thomas Hunt, Author of "The Custody Game" |
| Fee: | Free |
| Enrollment: | Limited to 50 |

(To reserve a seat, please call 555-2110)

At first glance, this event might appear to be a pro bono
undertaking.   The women and men who choose to attend are

likely to be divorced already, and, therefore, are not in need of the services of a divorce mediator. Clients will not come directly from the seminar audience.

Good will, a crucial element in any public relations program, is likely to be established by the sponsorship, however. In addition, word of mouth may lead to a new clientele. That is - audience members may tell their friends and associates about the seminar and the impressive divorce mediator who sponsored the program and spoke there.

More immediate and dramatic results can be expected, however, from press coverage of the event. A press release should be sent to local newspapers several weeks in advance, announcing the event, describing it and pointing out that it is free to the public. A public service announcement, containing the same information, should be sent to local radio and television stations.

The seminar is also an opportunity for local talk and news show appearances. The upcoming seminar provides, what reporters refer to as, a "news peg," a logical reason for a guest's appearance on radio or TV at this particular time.

Media coverage of the event should be encouraged too. Newspaper, magazine and broadcast representatives should be invited to attend and/or cover the seminar. Some follow-up publicity is likely to result.

The seminar is a good opportunity to seek some national media coverage. Although the event is hardly a major national news story, the advice given to attendees by the experts is the sort of guidance many magazine editors look for and like to pass along to readers. For this purpose, a summary of each speaker's remarks might be put into a feature, press release form and mailed to editors or managing editors of relevant national magazines. In order to gain visibility, the sponsoring mediator may wish to put his or her remarks first, or to devote more space to his or her remarks than to others. However, it is advisable to include remarks from all the experts in the mailing. It adds credibility to both the seminar and the mailing.

Even if this mailing results in little or no actual coverage, it benefits the mediator by putting his or her name in front of national editors. Editors may keep the releases on file for months or years, and may refer back to them in the future when a quote or information from a divorce expert is needed.

Ideally, the seminar program will have consisted of one short presentation by each expert, followed by a question and answer session with the audience. Both the presentations and the interchanges should be taped so that a transcript can be made. Then, in addition to the summaries of remarks, a list of selected questions and answers might be mailed to editors as well. A good angle to take when writing up the questions and answers in a press release for editors is something like: "The questions women are asking about divorce, and single parenthood."

In addition to organizing your own seminars, you may wish to participate in seminars sponsored by other professionals and/or organizations. In fact, speaking at an educational forum devoted to a more general topic may be more likely to result directly in the acquisition of new clients - simply because people, who are married but considering divorce, are more likely to be part of a general population audience.

## Studies

"A new study shows that ....."

Hundreds of news stories begin this way, whether the topic is as serious as infection rates for AIDS, or as subjective as public attitudes toward a political candidate's honesty or lack of it. Major studies and national polls normally involve large numbers of subjects or respondents. Statisticians normally consider 1,100 people the minimum number for a high, validity study in which the results are not predictable from the beginning.

Many good academic and business studies, however, are done locally and with many fewer subjects. The divorce mediator, who hopes to make genuine news, can benefit from conducting a small scale study of his or her own, then releasing the results to the press.

Research may be done by mailed questionnaire, by personal interviews with clients or their relatives, by direct observation in a controlled setting or by any number of other methods. Appropriate topics for study are myriad. Possibilities include the following:

- What topics cause the greatest disagreement in divorce mediation sessions? (finances, real estate, custody, visitation, etc.)
- What topics are the easiest on which to reach an agreement?
- What appeals to people most about divorce mediation? (Perhaps, comparing attitudes of those who have used mediation to those who have not.)
- How do attitudes toward second divorces differ from attitudes toward first divorces?
- Among college students, what percentage expect to marry only once? (compared to those who expect to be divorced at least one.)
- How do attitudes about a divorce and one's ex-spouse change over the course of time? (time of separation, time of divorce decree, three months after decree, six months after decree, etc. -- a longitudinal study.)
- How do children perceive divorce mediation? (surveying sons and daughters of couples who have gone through it.)

Rather than (or in addition to) publishing complete details of the study in an academic or professional journal, the divorce mediator should send a press release summarizing the results to his or her usual media mailing list. Such a release could be of interest to both local and national media.

## Sample Press Release on a Study

Contact: (404)555-3912
For Release On or After May 1, 1995

New Study Shows that Divorce Mediation
Leads to Fewer Fights, More Phone Calls

If you've got to get divorced, and you want to stay friends with your ex-spouse, then don't call a lawyer - call a mediator. That's what the results of a new study done by Atlanta divorce mediator and psychologist, Mary Booth Lowe, says.

Lowe surveyed more than one hundred divorced women and men in the Atlanta area, fifty of whom had reached their agreements through mediation, and fifty of whom had gone through a traditional litigated divorce with separate attorneys. The period of time since a divorce decree ranged from three months to two years.

Couples, who had gone through mediation, were almost twice as likely to describe their relationship with their ex-spouses as good or very good (no one described their relationship as excellent), and far less likely to describe the relationship as poor or horrible. Although minor disagreements occurred at about the same rate for people, who had been through mediation, and those, who had gone through litigated divorce, the former reported almost thirty percent fewer major disagreements. And although there was no significant difference between the two groups in how often they saw their ex-husbands and ex-wives face to face, the people who had been through mediation reported a much higher frequency of telephone contact.

"A reassuring number of people reported that they've actually become friends with their ex-husbands or ex-wives, and the phone is the major source of contact," Lowe notes. "Divorce mediation may not be the only factor responsible for this, but it's a very good indicator that people involved in it are doing something right."

Lowe, who holds a Ph.D. in clinical psychology from the University of Alabama, is a past president of the Georgia Chapter of the Academy of Family Mediators.

Detailed reports of the study are available from Lowe, Haskins & Associates, 2815 New Spring Road, Suite 115, Atlanta, GA 30339.

###

## Series of Feature Releases

A press release describing the results of new research is an example of a news release.  When a divorce mediator publishes a book or takes on a new partner, a release written about it is considered a news release since it reports on an actual event.

For most professionals, however, most publicity must be sought on the basis of feature articles, rather than news stories.  The distinction between the two is relatively simple.  If a Paris designer shows short skirts at a particular fashion show, that is a news story.  If women have begun to wear short skirts in America, a story, describing and analyzing that trend, is a feature.

Once the press has been sent the mediator's biography, photo and general press release, the mediator should not subside his or her efforts to send press releases on a regular basis in order to make the editor aware of the mediator's existence.  There is no hard and fast rule about the number of press releases that should be produced annually.  It is safe to say, however, that no small professional practice ever would need to distribute releases more often than one per month.  For most mediators, quarterly mailings should be sufficient to build and maintain visibility.

Although feature releases are, by definition, not "hard news," it can be advantageous to tie in their subjects with the season or with other events in order to create a sense of timeliness.  Possible topics for a mediator's feature press releases are as follows:

- New Year's Resolutions for the Divorced (January)
- The Romance of Pre-Nuptial Agreements! Thinking Ahead to the Divorce (February for Valentine's Day)
- Divorced Mothers Learn to Play Multiple Roles (May for Mother's Day)
- Moms without Custody: Breaking Tradition (May for Mother's Day)

- Dads without Custody: Finding Ways to Stay Close to their Children (June for Father's Day)
- For Father's with Custody, It's a New Lifestyle (June for Father's Day)
- Wedding Etiquette for the Serial Monogamist (June, traditional month for weddings)
- Got Custody for the Summer? Here's How to Make the Most of It (June or July for summer vacation)
- Holiday Dinners: The Challenge of Organizing the "New Family" (November for Thanksgiving or December for Christmas)
- The Return of Civility: Friendly Divorces Win Favor (any time of year might be tied in with a news story about a celebrity divorce)
- Lawyers as Divorce Mediators Play the Role of Nice Guys -- For a Change (any time of year might be tied in with a bar association news story, an anniversary or local event of some kind, or a media phenomenon such as the awarding of an Emmy to "L.A. Law" or some other attorney-connected program)
- How Divorce Lawyers and Mediators Stay Happily Married (any time of year)

Most feature releases will be based on the mediator's experience with clients, perhaps utilizing actual case histories and interviews with them. All feature releases will prominently feature quotes by the divorce mediator himself or herself. Divorce mediators able to afford professional public relations services will have the advantage of professional writers as part of the package.

You may want to use the material directly from this book; or, if your budget permits, the use of a professional freelance writer still may be worth the expenditure. National organizations such as the New York based American Society of Journalists and Authors can help mediators locate professional writers who live and work in or near their city. Another alternative is to seek out a local newspaper reporter or public relations department employee (many hold full time jobs and accept freelance writing assignments in their spare time).  Colleges and universities can be sources of help as well.  The Journalism, Public Relations or Communications Department offices may be willing to post a bulletin about your need for free lance help.  Writing fees vary widely, but are generally negotiated in terms of the length of the finished assignment, rather than by the day or hour.

The question of who should be the "contact" name on press releases is an important consideration for the individual mediator working without outside public relations counsel. Normally, a publicist's name is used.  The name of a secretary or assistant with good communication skills can be written on the release so that editors and broadcasters can ask him or her for additional information or to arrange an interview with the mediator.  If this is not a viable solution for your office, it may be best to list a contact telephone number with no name; media people will most likely ask for the mediator directly when calling.

## Miscellaneous

The public relations tools available to and appropriate for the professional are almost as varied as those used by large corporations when selling their products or services.  Attorneys publicizing their firms' services are advised to consider dozens of vehicles, including client newsletters, firm brochures, client dinners at partners' homes (Curtis and Atkins 1987), networking through political and civic activities (Shartsis 1987), the use of outside public relations firms and the individual promotion of "star" lawyers (Practicing Law Institute 1987).

Divorce mediators in private and group practice must consider all these possibilities in order to market their services successfully.  Although this section has been addressed to the individual mediator, the same guidelines apply to group practices.  Individual mediators within the practice should have their own biographies and photos included in press kits, and their quotes and experiences should be used in both news and feature releases. This approach personalizes both the firm and the service provided and is designed to build clientele for the individual as well as the group.

# CHAPTER 6

## What You Should Know about the Media

While it is vital to know the audience, it's also important to know as much as you can about the individual interviewer or reporter.

Newspaper reporters have opinions and attitudes about issues which can determine how a subject will be treated in print and the kinds of information the reporter will want. Television and radio interviews are governed by the same principles. The types of questions, the way they are asked and their tone can be based on any opinions they bring to the interview.

Broadcasters also have show formats and styles of interviewing. Some are hard-nosed interviewers seeking an expose, others are low-keyed and merely want to explore a subject. Therefore, it's important for you to know about the interviewer before you meet for an interview. There are several ways you can do this.

To learn the editorial attitudes of magazines and newspaper reporters, scan recent issues for their articles. Back copies of publications are usually available in public libraries, and newspapers have their own "morgue" files. These can give you ideas on how reporters have treated past issues, as well as patterns of their writing.

Broadcast shows should be viewed or heard prior to your participation.  Be alert to the interviewer's approach to his/her guests, tone, style of questioning, and attitudes toward issues.  The moderator's handling of opponents should be studied if the program format brings persons with varying views together on the same show.  Study alternate positions and opinions before appearing on the show.

Personal appearances at meetings of clubs or other groups should follow the same principles.  Thoroughly review data on the goals, interests and accomplishments of the organization beforehand.  This will help structure your speech and prepare for questions.

## Interviews with Print Media

Here are some suggestions which may help you to have a successful interview with the press:

1. Prepare your material.  Because of deadline pressure, have all facts, figures, and references on hand.  Have a written statement to hand out.

2. Anticipate key questions and have answers ready.  Know the WHO, WHAT, WHERE, WHEN, WHY, if appropriate, for major subject areas before the interview.

3. Express your points clearly, sharply, quickly and briefly.  This not only drives the main points home, but speeds up the interview.

4. Use concrete, not abstract words.  Try to create images to make your point clear.    Anecdotes, examples and case histories are useful in helping the publication's reader to visualize your point.

5. Provide as much background material as possible.  If it is supplied beforehand, it saves the interviewer a lot of time especially on complex issues.  If in-depth questions arise during an interview, which can be

answered with on-hand material, offer it.

6. Try to have interviews on a face-to-face basis, rather than over the phone. Personal contact is still the best means of communication.

7. If you promise additional information, follow up immediately. This includes printed material, or the names and telephone numbers of other possible interview sources.

8. When you have given all the necessary information, stop. It's appreciated by the reporter on a deadline, and it prevents needless talk just for the sake of keeping a conversation going.

## Things You Should Try to Avoid

1. Don't be too much of a salesperson.

2. Don't make up anything. If you don't have an answer readily at hand simply say "I'm not in a position at this time to say; may I get back to you on that."

3. Don't give any misleading information.

4. Don't do anything which might be interpreted as coercion, influence, or control of the content of the article. This includes asking the reporter what he or she will do with the information.

5. Don't criticize a reporter's writing style or argue about his/her handling of a topic. If a journalist asks you to check the facts in the material he has prepared -- just check the facts.

6. Don't say anything that you don't want to see in print. There is no such thing as "off the record" since a reporter can always attribute your

information to "a source close to the subject."

## Interviews with Radio and Television Media

The following are suggestions for your interviews with radio and television reporters:

1. Before you go on any program, prepare in advance two or three key ideas you want to get across. This is especially important since there is always a time constraint.

2. Anticipate key questions which may come up during the interview and be prepared to use those key questions as launching pads for your communication objectives.

3. Anticipate potentially negative questions and prepare points about them that can be turned into positive responses.

4. Try to end every answer regarding the subject of divorce with Mediation.

5. Always tell the truth.

6. Crystallize your ideas into a few short, hard-hitting phrases that summarize the essence of what you're trying to communicate. Remember radio and television are condensed media.

7. Use anecdotes whenever possible. Stories dramatize your point. However, they should be to the point and interesting.

8. Keep your voice, especially on radio, at an even pace. Try to think in terms of being at home and talking to a friend.

9. Preview a program before you appear so that you can observe the style, length of time guests appear, and the general tone the interviewer takes toward their guests -- friendly or hostile.

10. Get into the habit of using the interviewer's name in response to at least one question. But be careful of overdoing this.

11. Unless instructed don't look into the camera. Look directly at your moderator. The camera will follow you.

12. Don't be afraid to say "I don't know," if, in fact, you don't know. Be prepared to paraphrase what you've heard from other experts, and explain frankly that your specialty is in another area, if that's the case.

13. No matter how hostile an interviewer might become, don't get emotional or upset.

14. Don't let someone else put words in your mouth. If a reporter tries to rephrase your answer and distorts it, make it clear that the interviewer is quoting or interpreting your reply incorrectly. Restate your answer.

15. Listen carefully to the question and, if you don't understand, do not hesitate to ask the interviewer to repeat it.

16. Always be concerned, especially if you are answering calls from listeners.

## Speeches and Live Presentations

Here are some guidelines on developing and delivering your presentations:

1. Try to get advance information about your audience. Try to prepare your remarks with their interests in mind.

2. Decide what topics you want to discuss and what information you want to give the audience.

3. Before writing, give careful thought to your presentation, particularly your introduction, body of text, and conclusion. Be particularly aware of the time you are allotted and make sure your presentation fits into that time frame. Give enough time for questions.

4. Write for the ear. The audience will never see your words. Always think of how you will sound. What may read well on paper may sound dull or pedantic. Remember language's strength lies in nouns and verbs, not adjectives.

5. Give your audience only one idea at a time. Sentence structure should accentuate one image or idea, not an assortment. Use simple, short, declarative sentences.

6. Create images. We learn through our senses. The more vivid the images you create, the more the audience will become involved in what you are saying. Avoid abstractions. Citing examples and personal experiences will help the audience relate to your message.

## Rehearse Your Presentation

1. Practice aloud until you are able to give at least 80 per cent of the talk without using notes.

2. Underline key words. When you practice, emphasize important words by pausing just before them and raising or lowering the pitch of your voice as you say them. The rest of your thoughts can be delivered

much more quickly since they are less important.

3.  Use a tape recorder, while you practice, to hear how you sound.

4.   Use energy. Your audience will be with you, if you reach out to them.  Be passionate about your cause.

5.  When you have finished, don't forget to stop for a few seconds just to smile at your audience and thank them.

6. Most important HAVE FUN.

# CHAPTER 7

## Epilogue

As I come to the end of this book, I am far more optimistic than when I started. Even though the problems and limitations of successfully marketing divorce mediation are myriad and clear, the widespread acceptance of divorce mediation may not be immediately at hand. However, there are some positive indicators.

It seems that more attorneys are becoming involved in mediation in a variety of ways. They are incorporating it into their practices, giving up the practice of adversarial law for the non-adversarial approach, forming partnerships with mediators and working with social scientists in alliances which utilize the expertise of both professionals.

The program, which I have outlined, is only one combination of media and messages that might be used to further the cause of divorce mediation. Or it may be the first full scale effort of many to come.

As others have suggested, the initiation of a divorce ritual may be a giant step in the right direction. Just, as funerals celebrate the life of the deceased; it is, at the same time, a period of mourning for the loss of the person. A divorce rite could mark the death of a marriage, while honoring the good that came of it, and celebrating the beginning of an "afterlife" of sorts.

Since I began this project, the imminent introduction of a new national magazine on divorce has been announced in the press. This periodical, and the competitors, which are sure to follow it, if successful, may provide excellent new vehicles for communicating mediation's message.

Few public relations efforts can be all things to all people. This one has been designed with the upper-middle class consumer with his or her tastes and needs in mind. This upscale market was the one represented by participants in the Kindred Spirits survey, and it is likely to be a highly desirable market from the mediator's point of view.

But the needs of middle, lower-middle, and lower class consumers must be addressed as well. Certainly if a sample of divorced men and women in lower socio-economic brackets had completed the Kindred Spirits survey, many of their responses might have been different. They might have answered that cost was indeed a major consideration in the selection of an attorney. Then, if a public relations program were designed to target this audience, the relatively low cost of mediation would be given far greater emphasis.

It is always necessary to make a choice, when shaping a message for a particular audience rather than for all possible consumers. I chose to target a consumer group higher on the socio-economic scale at least partially because, through this group, it is most likely to capture the attention of and eventually win acceptance of consumers from virtually all socio-economic levels. Although there are occasional exceptions most social changes win acceptance from the top down, rather than the reverse.

When divorce mediation becomes a standard in America's curriculum, as I hope it will, it will be taught with its own set of assumptions and values. Surely students will be taught that it is better to solve problems by talking them out than by the use of force or violent argument.

The day when the study of conflict resolution begins in high school or college and when prestigious universities award degrees in mediation, will be the day when the process of divorce mediation will no longer need to be publicized in a formal sense. It will be a known alternative and individuals either will accept it or reject it on the basis of that knowledge and familiarity.

No matter what the future holds for the acceptance, practice, and evolution of divorce mediation, I will stand behind the position that there is such a thing as a good divorce. Perhaps some marriages should never have taken place, and it is better for everyone involved that they are ending. Perhaps some divorces will be handled intelligently, sensitively and fairly, and, therefore, can be labeled "successful." In many cases, both spouses and their children are happier with their lives after a divorce and may even have better relationships with each other as a result.

None of this can erase the fact, however, that separation, by its very nature, involves loss. Loss is a form of change. And we have learned that human beings react poorly to change, whether it is positive, negative or neutral, and no matter how smoothly it may be executed.

No one would wish the pain of an unhappy marriage and a divorce on a friend or loved one, although the experiences sometimes seem almost inevitable in our culture. If and when mediation is widely accepted and used, at least, we can wish them the smoothest possible transition and the best new lives.

# APPENDIX I

## Summary of Survey Results

### DEMOGRAPHICS

| | | |
|---|---|---|
| AVERAGE AGE | | 41 |
| AVERAGE AGE AT MARRIAGE | | 25 |
| AVERAGE LENGTH OF MARRIAGE | | 12 years |
| AVERAGE TIME SINCE DIVORCE | | 4 years |
| | | |
| NUMBER OF CHILDREN | One | 42.8% |
| | Two | 43.3% |
| | Three | 10.3% |
| | Four-Six | 1.3% |
| | None | 2.3% |
| | | |
| AVERAGE NUMBER OF CHILDREN | | 1.67 |

1. Occupation

## MOST COMMON CAREER FIELDS

### Men
| | |
|---|---|
| Professor, Teacher, Principle | 11.4% |
| Physician, Dentist, Psychologist | 11.4% |
| Marketing, Advertising and Computer fields | 10.3% |
| Attorney | 9.1% |

### Women
| | |
|---|---|
| Teacher, Administrator, Counselor | 20.9% |
| Nursing, Psychology/Psychiatry | 16.0% |
| Secretary, Executive secretary,<br>  Administrative assistants | 10.2% |
| Advertising, Marketing, Personnel,<br>  Public relations, Computer systems | 9.2% |
| Real estate, Management | 4.9% |
| Attorney | 4.4% |

2. Last divorce was your

| | |
|---|---|
| FIRST | 87.5% |
| SECOND | 11.6% |
| THIRD | 0.8% |

3. Before you decided to end your relationship with your spouse, did you see a therapist, counselor or clergyman?

| | |
|---|---|
| AS A COUPLE | 26.4% |
| ALONE | 19.0% |
| NO | 23.2% |
| ALONE AND AS A COUPLE | 31.4% |

4. Did the therapist, counselor, or clergyman suggest mediation?

| | |
|---|---|
| YES | 10.2% |
| NO | 89.8% |

5. If the answer is yes, please designate which professional suggested mediation.

| | |
|---|---|
| THERAPIST | 82.1% |
| COUNSELOR | 17.9% |
| CLERGYMAN | 0% |

6. While negotiating your separation and divorce, did you feel your former spouse was

| | |
|---|---|
| FAIR | 28.9% |
| UNREASONABLE | 22.7% |
| IRRATIONAL | 38.9% |
| OTHER | 9.5% |

7. How did you find your lawyer?

| | |
|---|---|
| REFERRAL (from friend or relative) | 64.6% |
| ADVERTISEMENT | 4.6% |
| ANOTHER LAWYER | 11.1% |
| NO LAWYER | 2.4% |
| OTHER | 18.4% |

8. Was cost a factor in your choice of lawyer?

| | |
|---|---|
| YES | 40.8% |
| NO | 59.2% |

9. Did you interview more than one lawyer?

|  |  |
|---|---|
| YES | 43.8% |
| NO | 56.2% |

10. What do you think someone contemplating a divorce should look for when choosing a lawyer? (Figures after each quality represent number of times that quality was mentioned.)

| | |
|---|---|
| DIVORCE SPECIALIST | 232 |
| EMPATHETIC | 149 |
| NEGOTIATOR | 126 |
| BUSINESSLIKE | 54 |
| ADVERSARIAL | 44 |
| ACCESSIBLE | 39 |
| SAME SEX | 36 |
| PROTECT CLIENT INTEREST | 33 |
| HONEST | 27 |
| GOOD REPRESENTATIVE | 26 |
| NON-ADVERSARIAL | 15 |
| EFFICIENT | 14 |
| REASONABLY PRICED | 9 |
| OTHER | 7 |

11. How important was your lawyer in the final outcome?

|  |  |
|---|---|
| NOT IMPORTANT | 43.2% |
| IMPORTANT | 56.8% |

12. Did your lawyer pressure you into an agreement?

|  |  |
|---|---|
| YES | 20.4% |
| NO | 79.6% |

13. Did your lawyer discuss mediation with you?

    YES                         16.1%
    NO                          83.9%

14. Would you recommend your attorney to another person going
    through a divorce?

    YES                         58.5%
    NO                          41.5%

15. Did your have a court trial on the issue of your divorce?

    YES                         17.0%
    NO                          71.5%
    PENDING                     11.5%

16. Did your involvement with the legal process make your
    relationship with your spouse more difficult?

    YES                         54.2%
    NO                          45.8%

17. Before you sought out a lawyer, had you heard about
    mediation?

    YES                         45.6%
    NO                          54.4%

18. Before you read the pamphlet enclosed, would you have known
    where to find a mediator?

    YES                         39.8%
    NO                          60.2%

19. Do your think you and your former spouse could have worked out the terms of separation and divorce with the help of a professional divorce mediator?

|  |  |
|---|---|
| POSSIBLY | 48.2% |
| NO | 34.7% |
| YES | 17.1% |

20. If not, why do you feel you could not have used mediation?

|  |  |
|---|---|
| ATTITUDE/BEHAVIOR OF SPOUSE | 61 mentions |
| NEED FOR LAWYER/COURT SYSTEM | 28 |
| COMPLEX LEGAL/FINANCIAL ISSUES | 14 |
| AMICABLE DIVORCE/SIMPLE ISSUES | 10 |
| ATTITUDE/BEHAVIOR OF BOTH SPOUSE AND SELF | 7 |

21. Would you advise a friend who is considering divorce to use a mediator?

|  |  |
|---|---|
| YES | 69.1% |
| NO | 11.2% |
| NOT SURE | 3.8% |
| DEPENDS ON THE SITUATION | 15.8% |

# APPENDIX II

## Explanation of Survey Results

The questionnaire (pp. 139-142) asked for basic demographical information: sex, age, number of children, occupation, number of divorces and the number of years that the subject had been married, separated and divorced.

The average age of all subjects was 41. The average person answering the survey had married at age 25, remained married for 12 years and had been divorced four years at the time of the study.

Averages differed somewhat for male and female subjects. The average age for men was 45 and had been married for an average of 14 years. The average female subject was 39 years old and had been married 11 years.

The average number of children among respondents was 1.67. More than 86 percent of those responding reported having either one or two children. Approximately ten percent reported having three. Only 1.3 percent reported having four of more.

No one had more than six.  And although Kindred Spirits is promoted as an organization for parents, nine people (2.3 percent) reported having no children at all.

The vast majority of survey participants (86.9 percent of men, 88 percent of women) had gone through only one divorce. More than 11 percent of both men and women had been divorced twice.  Only three subjects, all male, reported having been divorced three times.  That figure represented 1.8 percent of all men responding to this question, and 0.8 percent of all responses.

A wide range of occupations were reported among both sexes.  Of the 175 men who answered the question, "What kind of work do you do?," the greatest number worked in education, health services, business services and law.

Twenty subject (11.4 percent) reported job titles of professor, teacher or principal, ranging from grade school to university level.  An additional 20 (11.4 percent) described themselves as physicians, dentists, psychologists or with other health care titles.  Of those in the business services category (18 subjects, 10.3 percent), most were in marketing, advertising and computer fields.  All 16 subjects (9.1 percent) in the legal field were attorneys.

Other occupational fields represented by the men in the study included communications, electrical and electronic equipment, the textile industry, banking and finance, building contracting, publishing, accounting, real estate and public administration.

For the 206 women who responded to the question about work, the fields of education and health were even more dominant.  Forty-three (20.9 percent) fell into the category of educational services.  The greatest number were teachers, followed by administrators, counselors, and other educational specialists.  Thirty-three (16 percent) of the subjects worked in health care, 12 in nursing and 10 in psychology/psychiatry.

Office services accounted for the career of 21 (10.2 percent) subjects.  Ten described themselves as secretaries, executive secretaries or administrative assistants.  Almost as many women (19 subjects, or 9.2 percent) were in business service. Career fields within this category included advertising marketing, personnel, public relations and computer systems. Ten (4.9 percent) subjects were in real estate sales or management. Nine (4.4 percent) were attorneys.

Other occupational fields represented by the women in the study included public administration, retail trade and the textile and food service industries. Only four subjects (1.9 percent) described themselves as homemakers.

No questions on educational level or income were included on the questionnaire. The careers listed, however, indicate above-average education and earning power for both the men and women who responded.


## Therapy, Counseling, and Mediation

The next three questions delved into the questions of pre-divorce counseling and whether the professionals involved in such sessions recommended divorce mediation.

Question 3 asked, "Before you decided to end your relationship with your spouse, did you see a therapist, counselor or clergyman?" Almost eight out of ten subjects (76.8) said they had sought such feedback. A full 76 percent of the men responding to this question and 78.4 percent of the women answered yes.

Women were more likely to report having seen the counselor alone, rather than going as a couple. Forty-nine women (24 percent of those responding) had sought counseling alone, compared with only 23 (13.1 percent) of the men. For all survey participants, the figure was 19 percent.

Men were more likely to report having gone into counseling as half a couple. Sixty-two males (35.4 percent) said they had seen a counselor, therapist, or clergyman only with their spouses. Of all survey participants, 26.4 percent said they had gone as a couple.

A substantial number reported having been counseled

under both circumstances. Seventy-three women (35.8 percent) and 46 men (26.3 percent) had seen some sort of counselor, both alone and as a couple. Overall, the figure was 31.4 percent.

Some subjects may have been seeing therapists or counselors before the break-ups of their marriages seemed apparent. A 48-year-old dentist clarified his situation by writing in a fourth category and checking it: "D. Was already seeing a therapist."

The others who checked no on this question may have discussed the end of the marriage at other points in time. A 35-year-old Optometry office manager and mother of one pointed out that she had seen a professional "afterwards and prior to the decision (during pregnancy)."

Overwhelmingly, the professionals they saw did not recommend divorce mediation to the individuals and/or couples involved. Of the 293 subjects who responded to question 4, only 30 (10.2 percent) reported that the person who counseled them had recommended the mediation process. A full 90.2 percent of men and 90.4 percent of women answered no to the question, "Did the therapist, counselor or clergyman suggest mediation?"

Of the approximately ten percent that did suggest mediation, the vast majority were therapists. Of the 28 instances in which mediation was recommended (note: two people did not identify the professional involved), 23 of those recommendations (82.1 percent) were made by therapists. Five (17.9 percent) were made by counselors. None at all were made members of the clergy.

## Descriptions of Spouse's Behavior During Divorce

Question 6 asked divorced men and women to characterize their spouses during the negotiations of their separation and divorce. "Were the now ex-husbands and ex-wives seen as fair, unreasonable, irrational or in some other way?"

More than sixty percent (228, or 61.6 percent) of all

respondents to this question viewed their spouses as unreasonable or irrational during separation and divorce negotiations. Women were slightly kinder than men in their recollections, with 58.9 percent describing their former husbands in one of those two ways. Other men responding to this question, 64.9 percent characterized their former wives with one of the two negative adjectives.

More women than men viewed their ex-spouses as having been fair during negotiations. Sixty-three women (31.2 percent) and 44 men (26.2 percent) used this description.

Irrational was the term chosen by the majority of those choosing one of the two unflattering descriptions. Seventy-nine women (39.1 percent) and 65 men (38.7 percent) checked the description "irrational." Forty-four men (26.2 percent) and 40 women (19.8 percent) checked "unreasonable" instead.

A considerable number -- 20 women (9.9 percent) and 15 men (8.9 percent) checked the description "other". Although the questionnaire did not ask them to elaborate, some subjects volunteered descriptions of their own or elaborated on those given on the form.

"It would change from day to day."
-- Electrical engineer
Male, age 37

"Other -- & worse."
-- Apparel firm president
Male, age 46

"Upset."
--Registered nurse
Female, age 39

"Both he and his attorney were unethical in their practices toward me during negotiation."
--Graphic artist

Female, age 42

"Vindictive."
--Pharmaceutical executive
Female, age 39

"Very irrational."
--Attorney
Male, age 37

"Irrational and insane."
--Teacher/psychotherapist
Female, age 37

"Greedy."
--Doctor
Male, age 43

"Mostly OK, considering the circumstances and
because of the children."
--University administrator
Female, age 39

"All at various times."
--Mother/teacher/nursing student
Female, age 32

"Unavailable."
--Attorney
Female, no age given

"Using blackmail."
--Advertising writer
Male, age 65

"Generally fair, but some irrationality
engendered by spouse's lack of business/

legal knowledge."
        --Attorney
        Male, age 44


"Unreasonable, Irrational, Dishonest, Greedy,
Abusive."
        --Writer/college professor
        Male, age 47


## Methods for Selection of Attorney

Question 7 asked the subjects how the lawyer they used during their divorce was found: by referral (through family or friends), as a result of seeing one or more advertisements, through another attorney or in some other way.

The majority of attorneys were found through referral. Of the 370 subjects who responded to this question, 239 (64.6 percent) had found their lawyers in this way. Women were more likely (69 percent) than men (59.5 percent) to have used referral.

As the discussion of correlation later in this section will indicate, such referrals were not always satisfactory. A 39-year-old marketing manager and father of one indicated this when he checked the answer, referral from a friend or relative, then wrote in parentheses: "Now x-friend".

In addition 41 of the attorneys (11.1 percent) were found through other attorneys -- a form of referral in itself. Combining these two figures, it might be said that three out of four (75.7 percent) of all divorce lawyers are hired as a result of referrals. Only a total of 17 respondents (4.6 percent) had chosen their attorneys as a result of advertising. Women were slightly more likely (5.1 percent) than men (4 percent) to hire a lawyer whose advertisements they had seen.

A considerable number (68, or 18.4 percent) of subjects reported having chosen their attorneys by other methods. Thirty-nine men (22.5 percent) and 29 women (14.7 percent) answered question 7 in this way. A number of subjects indicated that "other" meant choosing a relative or personal friend who was an attorney.    Old high school and college classmates were mentioned in several instances.  Others wrote:

> "My ex is a lawyer. We selected a mutual friend who did the divorce for free as a professional courtesy."
> > --Adverting copywriter
> > Female, no age given

> "We used the same attorney who was a friend."
> > --Educator
> > Female, age 50

Other subjects had chosen attorneys by reputation.

> "My wife picked a famous bomber....I was scared and picked another famous bomber. (I had read of their cases in The New York Times.)"
> > --Music Arranger
> > Male, age 46

> "Newspaper article."
> > --Pediatrician
> > Male, age 49

> "Three other divorce lawyers said he is the best."
> > --Investment banker
> > Male, age 39

It was not unusual for a subject to report having a regular attorney or at least to have worked with the divorce lawyer before on a different kind of case.

"She was my real estate lawyer."
                    --Real estate syndicator
                    Female, age 43


"Firm already handled my regular business."
                    --Money manager
                    Male, no age given


"Used same lawyer for different reason before."
                    --Hospital manager
                    Female, age 41


Business contacts accounted for several attorney-client relationships. One subject reported hiring an attorney who was a business client. Another chose a law firm that was close to his office. One woman chose the attorney that taught her law class.

There were several cases of therapist referrals to lawyers. Other subjects mentioned finding attorneys through the local bar association.


"I shopped local big firms."
                    -- Substitute teacher
                    Female, age 43


"Called around."
                    -- Psychologist
                    Male, age 41


"I....did a great deal of research.  Since I had
used a senile attorney during a previous separation
(who is eminent by senile unbeknownst to me). I
needed someone I could trust."
                    -- Consultant
                    Female, age 43


A number of subjects answered question 7 by explaining their minimal need for lawyers during the divorce process.

"My ex and I did a do-it-yourself divorce."
-- Professional
Male, age 39

"I filed my divorce myself."
--Secretary
Female, age 27

"We did not use attorneys! We worked it out alone!"

-- Real estate broker
Female, age 41

Nine subjects (2.9 percent of men, 2 percent of women and 2.4 percent of survey participants overall) reported having had no lawyer.


## Criteria for Selection of Attorney

The high cost of legal services apparently was not as great a factor as might have been expected. Almost six out of ten (215, or 59.2 percent) said that fees did not influence their choice of attorney. Women and men appeared to feel much the same way on this subject; 59.9 percent of men and 58.7 percent of women responded with a resounding no.

Several respondents volunteered comments on the subject.

"You bet.  In the end, it cost me $50,000 and I'm
still paying through the nose -- eight years later.
In fact, I changed lawyers in mid-course because the
first one turned out to be in it only for the bucks."
-- Psychology professor
Male, age 48

"Yes, but it still cost $20,000."
> -- Therapist
> Female, age 39

"Neither of us could remotely afford them.  She didn't pay hers.  I paid $10,000."
> -- Painter/substitute teacher
> Male, age 46

"Used divorce mediation.  Chose not to this route (lawyer) because of cost."
> -- Social Worker
> Female, age 42

"No. we discussed $ and I felt I could afford. If not, I would have gone to another."
> -- Library service director
> Female, age 43

"No. Nothing to compare."
> -- Professor
> Male, age 40

"No. But you get what you pay for!!"
> -- Marketing manager
> Male, age 39

Shopping around was relatively uncommon.  Only 160 (43.8 percent) of the 365 subjects who responded to this question reported having interviewed more than one lawyer.  Women (46.4 percent) were somewhat more likely than men (40.8 percent) to have interviewed two or more attorneys before choosing one to handle the divorce.

A 37-year-old male CPA reported having interviewed five attorneys.  A 56-year-old female teacher said she had interviewed three, and that "all were prejudiced against women." A 45-year-old sales manager, who had been a homemaker until her divorce, explained that she had not interviewed more than one attorney, but that she had switched to a divorce specialist at her first attorney's suggestion.

What did these men and women look for in a lawyer? More specifically, question 10 asks the subjects what " someone contemplating a divorce should look for when choosing a lawyer?" Suggestions mentioned in parentheses on the form itself were as follows: "same sex, specialize in divorce, adversarial, negotiator, empathetic and businesslike."


### Specialization, Empathy and Ability to Negotiate

According to 232 of the survey subjects, the attorney they chose for the divorce specialized in divorce law. (Note: Percentages of the total will not be mentioned in the discussion of this particular question, because most subjects gave multiple answers.) Specialization was the single criterion mentioned most often.

> "A matrimonial specialist who is a 'killer' and a
> negotiator at the same time.
> -- Sakes rep
> Male, age 51

The need for a lawyer who is empathetic came in second, with 149 mentions. Fourteen people also volunteered the adjective "understanding," which might be taken as a synonym for empathetic. Not all of those who hoped for empathy actually expected to find it in an attorney-client relationship. A father of two, divorced in 1985, circled the word empathetic on his questionnaire but wrote to the side, "Personally preferred. But humanity is irrelevant in litigation."

Negotiator came in third as the most desirable description of one's lawyer, with 126 mentions.

"Negotiator who can see destructive role adversarial
system promotes".
                    -- Social worker
                    Male, age 37

Of the six descriptions suggested on the questionnaire, same sex
was the description used by the fewest number of subjects. Only
36 (26 of whom were women) said they considered it important
that women be represented by a female attorney, and men by a
male. A 42-year-old female guidance counselor suggests
"someone who is pro-female and very tough".

Adversarial was the second least popular description.
Only 44 subjects said they considered this an important quality
for a lawyer. Fifteen subjects wrote in the description, "non-
adversarial."

Others may have felt that the term adversarial was not
strong enough.

"Someone who would go for the throat."
                    -- Travel agent
                    Female, age 42

"Hungry, nasty, mean, killer instinct, VN vet, go
for juggler (sic), etc. It appears as though most
lawyers favor representing the female -- easier
case to win and look like a 'hero.'"
                    -- Marketing manager
                    Male, age 39

Businesslike came in as third least important of the six suggested
descriptions, with 54 mentions. It may be tied in with other
qualities, however.

"One should....look for a business like individual
who can evaluate a particular situation and make
decisions or help plan a course of action that is

in the best interest of the client and children."
-- Reading specialist
Female, age 40

## Accessibility, Advocacy and Honesty

Perhaps even more significant are the qualities mentioned most often of those not suggested parenthetically on the questionnaire. The importance of accessibility was mentioned on a total of 39 questionnaires.

"Someone who's accessible, sympathetic to
particulars of case, smart, analytic (and
has) enough time".
-- Interior designer
Female, age 36

"Not too busy to follow through (ha!)"
-- Administrator
Female, age 36

The second most frequent voluntary comment was that the lawyer should be one who protects the client's interest. A total of 33 subjects volunteered this observation.

An additional 27 people commented that the lawyer should be honest. But as a 47-year-old engineer and father of two commented, "I'm afraid this is too much to hope for in a lawyer."

If disillusionment in and antagonism toward the legal profession is good for the growth and acceptance of divorce mediation, then the field's future may be bright indeed. Exclamation marks, underlinings and comments written in margins appear to be expressions of very negative feelings toward attorneys and the subjects' experiences with them.

A 39-year-old investment banker gave his questionnaire a headline by writing in Shakespeare's quote from King Henry

VI, Part II: "First...let's kill all the lawyers." Other comments that indicated negative images of the legal profession included the following:

> "I have a very poor opinion of lawyers. High-
> priced, give poor or no advice, dictators....."
> -- Self-employed
> Male, no age given

> "(A lawyer should be) empathetic, same sex,
> common sense, non-lawyer-like."
> -- University administrator
> Female, age 39

> "Someone interested in getting it done and not
> dragging it out to get more money."
> -- Engineer
> Male, age 41

> "Not seek to protract matters in order to
> increase fee!!"
> -- Self-employed
> Male, age 52

It should be noted that both these subjects had answered no to question 8, "Was cost a factor in your choice of lawyer?"

Even attorneys themselves had complaints about the system.

> "Someone who is ethical and fair but (has) the ability
> to be firm and unfair if his adversary persists (in)
> being intimidating. (This is what I believe happens
> most of the time -- Matrimonial lawyers unconsciously
> 'stir up' conflict."
> -- Attorney
> Male, age 53

## Attorney Described As Mediator

In several instances, subjects wrote in response to question 10 that sounded very much like descriptions of a mediator, rather than of an attorney.

> "Somebody who is capable of listening to your
> suggestions sometimes (After all, you know your
> ex-husband better than he does)."
> > -- Design office employee
> > Female, age 39

> "Someone who understands the emotional pressures
> and who is there to encourage a settlement --
> not litigation."
> > -- Attorney
> > Male, age 45

> "One who thinks of the well-being of parties involved."
> > -- Economist
> > Male, age 49

> "A straight shooter who looks out for both sides."
> > -- Executive
> > Male, age 38

> "(One who) understands that there are early consider-
> ations like guilt which should be dealt with before
> a settlement is made."
> > -- University administrator
> > Female, age 50

> "Negotiator who can see (the) destructive role
> adversarial system promotes, has interest in family,
> especially children, can see 'down the road'....
> Avoid lawyer who is 'out to get' someone."
> > -- Social worker

## Male, age 40

A 42-year-old father of three described a situation in which an attorney functioned very much as he might have if a mediator had been involved:

> "My ex-wife and I worked out the terms of our
> agreement, our (common) lawyer merely turned
> the substantive agreement into legal phrasing.

This man's basic answer to question 10 -- what to look for in a lawyer -- had been "non-antagonistic, non-adversarial, understanding, businesslike."

Question 10 also gave at least one subject the opportunity to describe mediation as welcome but imperfect:

> "We used divorce mediation.  I liked it at the
> time because it didn't create bitter adversarial
> feelings.  But I'm not so sure my best interests
> were served because he (my ex) was more aggressive
> and verbal."
>                    -- Registered nurse
>                    Female, age 35

### Male Versus Female Responses on Qualities of Lawyer

There were only relatively minor differences in the responses of men and women on what to look for in a lawyer.

A full 26 percent of all men and 27.9 percent of all women mentioned finding an attorney who specialized in divorce.  An empathetic lawyer was suggested by 18.2 percent of all women responding to this question, and 16.5 percent of all men. The ideal lawyer was described at least in part as a negotiator by 17 percent of the men and by 13 percent of the women.

A businesslike attorney was called for by 6.8 percent of

men and 6 percent of women. An adversarial attorney was sought by 5.7 percent of men and 4.8 percent of women. The description "non-adversarial" was written in by 2.2 percent of men and 1.4 percent of women. A need for accessibility was volunteered as a description by 5.1 percent of men and 4.1 percent of women. Honesty was valued by 3.5 percent of men and 2.9 percent of women. Experience was mentioned by 4.3 percent of men and 4.8 percent of women. The need for reasonably priced attorneys was noted by 1.1 percent of men and 1 percent of women. Efficiency was mentioned by 1.8 percent of men and 1.4 percent of women.

Female subjects did mention two qualities somewhat more often than did male. A good representative was called for by 4.3 percent of women and by 1.4 percent of men. A lawyer of the same sex as the client was recommended by 4.3 percent of women and 2.7 percent of men.

## Lawyer's Role in Divorce

Looking back on their divorce, subjects were asked in question 11, "How important was your lawyer to the final outcome?" Of the 317 subjects who answered this question, 56.8 percent said their lawyers had been important in the outcome of their divorces.

> "Ex-husband got everything & then some."
> -- Graphic artist
> Female, age 42

> "I did not have my own lawyer at the time of the divorce....I had to get a lawyer two years later to get a fair agreement. I was very naive."
> -- Psychologist
> Female, age 39

> "Ineffective. (A woman two years out of law

school was assigned me by _____.)"
                -- Music arranger
                Male, age 46

"Important immediately following separation and
divorce but since then my ex-husband and I have
worked out any amendments in the agreement."
                -- Certified Public Accountant
                Female, age 36

"Should have used her lawyer."
                -- Marketing executive
                Male, age 39

Slightly more than 43 percent, however, said their lawyers had
not been important.

"I am a man. If I had any sense, I should have
known that fighting to get joint custody was
a losing battle."
                -- Research scientist
                Male, age 48

"Judge important more than lawyer."
                -- Real estate investor
                Male, age 51

"Really only put our own negotiated agreement
into writing."
                -- Business owner
                Female, age 38

Male subjects assessed their attorneys' importance slightly higher
than did females. Almost six out of ten men (59.6 percent)
checked "important", as opposed to 54.2 percent of women.
        Question 12 asked subjects, "Did your lawyer pressure
you into an agreement?" Overall, the subjects reported not

feeling pressured. Of the 343 subjects who responded to this question, only 70 (20.4 percent) checked yes. There was virtually no gender difference in the response, with 79.9 percent of women reporting not having been pressured.

Several subjects, however, commented on the subject.

> "Not exactly, but I was not well informed as to best probable legal outcome and while my actions turned out for the best, they were not taken for right reasons."
> -- Secretary
> Female, age 44

> "Leaned."
> -- Restaurant owner
> Male, age 46

> "Tried to, but I held firm."
> -- Administrator
> Female, age 39

> "The judge did."
> -- Therapist
> Female, age 39

Overwhelmingly, attorneys did not bring up the topic of divorce mediation. To question 13, "Did your lawyer discuss mediation with you?," 298 of the 355 subjects responding (83.9 percent) answered no. Somewhat fewer women than men recalled the subject of mediation arising. A full 87 percent of female subjects checked no, compared to 80.4 percent of men.

> "He said it is worthless."
> -- Investment Banker
> Male, age 39

> "I consulted him and he said I should give it

a try if I wanted to."
             -- Bookkeeper
             Female, age 39


Perhaps the acid test for lawyer satisfaction is question 14, "Would you recommend your attorney to another person going through a divorce?" By a reasonable margin, the answer is yes. Of 349 people responding to this question, 204 (58.5 percent) said they would recommend their attorneys to others. Men reported a somewhat higher recommendation rate than women. Of the male subjects, 61.2 percent checked yes to question 14; only 56.1 percent of women did so.

The issue brought out a variety of reactions, ranging from sincere enthusiasm to sarcasm.

"He _is_ the best in my area."
             -- Investment Banker
             Male, age 39

"Only as an adversarial."
             -- Unemployed administrator
             Female, age 38

"Absolutely."
             -- Accessories designer
             Female, age 35

"Yes -- to a millionaire or super Yuppie."
             -- Painter/plasterer
             Male, age 46

"Only if he/she wanted a loser."
             -- Orthopedics manager
             Male, age 39

## **Effects of the Court System/Legal Process**

Relatively few divorces result in court trials, according to the results of this survey. Of the 358 subjects who answered question 15, "Did you have a court trial on the issues of your divorce?," only 61 (17 percent) said yes. That represents 17.8 percent of men responding to the question, and 16.4 percent of woman. A full 73 percent of men and 70.3 percent of women reported not having gone to trial.

To those who did, however, and even to those who only came close, memories seemed vivid.

> "4 days over 8 months!"
> -- Accountant
> Male, age 46

> "Up to Superior Court."
> -- Office manager
> Female, age 45

> "No. Almost, though. Settled on day of trail."
> -- Certified public accountant
> Male, age 37

> "I threw in the towel on the court house steps."
> -- Scientist
> Male, age 48

More than 11 percent answered by explaining that their cases were pending. That answer was given by 9.2 percent of men and 13.3 percent of women.

Subjects were next asked Question 16, "Did your involvement with the legal process make your relationship with your spouse more difficult?"

Men reported their relationships damaged more often than did women. Of 162 men responding to this question, 102 (63 percent) checked yes. Of 187 women responding, 87 (46.5

percent) checked yes.  Overall, 54.2 percent of those responding reported believing that their relationship with their ex-spouses had been hurt.

"In a way.  He was used to always getting his way."
            -- Teacher
            Female, no age given

"More difficult as compared to what.  WW II?"
            -- Marketing executive
            Male, age 35

"You bet....I could go on!!"
            -- Professor
            Male, age 45

"At first, but not long term."
            -- Group controller
            Male, age 38

"We only got through it by minimizing (sic) the lawyer's roles, negotiating between ourselves mostly."
            -- Entrepreneur
            Female, age 40

"Couldn't get more difficult."
            -- Director
            Male, age 32

"Nothing could make it worse."
            -- Economist
            Female, age 39

"A thousand times yes!"
            -- Physician
            Male, age 47

"!!!!!"
           -- Stock broker
           Male, age 41


## Awareness of and Opinions on Divorce Mediation

Question 17 asked, "Before you sought out a lawyer, had you heard about mediation?" of 364 people responding to the question, 166 (45.6 percent) said they had heard of mediation beforehand. Women were more likely to report never having heard of the process, with 41.9 percent answering yes and 58.1 percent answering no. Men were divided exactly 50-50, with 83 subjects answering yes and 83 answering no.

One subject volunteered this information:

"And I used one -- but I refused to sign the
final papers."
           -- Teacher
           Female, age 42

Subjects were next asked, Question 18, "Before you read the pamphlet enclosed, would you have known where to find a mediator?" Approximately 40 percent (146 of 367, 39.8 percent) of those responding to the question said no. Again, women were slightly more likely to report or confess to ignorance of the subject. Only 37.4 percent checked yes to this question compared with 42.6 percent of men.

One woman noted how she had come to hear of the process:

"Subsequently found out about mediation available
in my county through therapist friends."
           -- Business owner
           Female, age 40

Question 19 and 20 asked subjects to reflect on their experiences and assess the possible benefits of having used mediation. To the first question, "Do you think you and your former spouse could have worked out the terms of separation and divorce with the help of a professional family mediator?," roughly two out of three subjects answered "yes" or "possibly".

The definite yes answers were outnumbered ·by the answers of possibly almost three to one, however. Of 369 subjects responding to question 19, only 63 (17.1 percent) checked yes. A total of 178 (48.2 percent) checked possibly. The remaining 128 (34.7) percent answered no.

Combining the two positive answers, women's and men's responses were strikingly similar. Approximately 66.6 percent of all men answered yes or possibly. As did 64.2 percent of women.

Breaking those answers down, however, men's responses appeared to be more definite than women's. Of the male subjects, 77 (45.8 percent) answered possibly and 35 (20.8 percent) answered yes. Of the female subjects 101 (50.2 percent) answered possibly and only 28 (13.9 percent) answered yes.

### Opinions: Why Mediation Wouldn't Have Worked

Those subjects who answered no to question 19 were asked to explain their responses in question 20: "If not, why do you feel you could not have used mediation?"

Of the 128 who had checked "definitely not" on question 19, 114 (52 men and 62 women) responded to this question. As in the case of question 10, multiple answers were common. Percentages will be noted, but will add up to more than 100 percent.

By far, the most common response to question 20 was to place the blame on the ex-spouse. A total of 61 subjects (53.5 percent) mentioned the ex-spouse's attitudes or behavior as a reason that mediation would not have worked. Women were more likely than men to mention this. A total of 39 women (62.9

percent) gave a spouse behavior or attitude reason, as opposed to 22 men (42.3 percent).

The most commonly cited attitude problem in this category was "spouse irrational/unreasonable." The second most common situation was one in which the spouse was simply unavailable; either he or she refused involvement with the process, didn't want the divorce or had abandoned the other spouse and was nowhere to be found. A total of nine women (including all the mentions of abandonment) and six men mentioned this situation.

Spouses described as angry, vengeful or vindictive came in third. Inflexible spouses came in fourth. Three women noted spouses who were violent or otherwise abusive. Other descriptions mentioned included spouses who were drug addicts or alcoholics, resentful, immature, inequitable/unfair and dishonest.

> "She is intransigent, litigious and wrapped up in her own rage. She has blackmailed me and brainwashed my children."
> -- Music arranger
> Male, age 46

> "My ex-husband was violent, lying, cheating. Tried to destroy my professional reputation and the relationship between me and my son. You cannot mediate with a lying fool."
> -- Chiropractor
> Female, age 35

> "Because I was married to an Iranian psychologist whose vocabulary does not include the word 'equitable', which is the basic function of a mediator. P.S. He does pre-divorce mediation in his private practice. Now you explain that one!!!"
> -- Professor
> Female, age 35

"It takes two to mediate."
> -- College Professor
> Male, age 46

Subjects were far less likely to attribute these kinds of attitudes to themselves as well. Only seven questionnaires (6.1 percent) attributed guilt for negative attitudes or behaviors to the subjects and their spouses. Women were slightly more likely to accept responsibility in this area, with 7.7 percent of all responses falling into this category. Only 4.8 percent of all male subjects' responses did so.

Some comments in this category: "no spirit of working it out," "too emotionally heated," "both not ready to be reasonable," "too angry to talk," "personality clash," "both of us inflexible."


## Mediators: In the Shadow of Lawyers

After attributing blame to the spouse, the most common reason given for not using mediation was the presence of lawyers -- personally or in a more abstract way. A total of 28 questionnaires (24.6 percent) mentioned issues surrounding attorneys and the legal system.

Women were considerably more concerned about this issue than men, with 19 female subjects (30.6 percent) mentioning this area. A substantial number of men, however, nine subjects, (17.3 percent) mentioned it as well.

In eleven cases, the subject expressed a need for an attorney and/or the legal system. It was noted that mediation is not legally binding and that the court system offers certain protection that mediation does not.

It should be noted, however, that three of the eleven questionnaires that fell into this category were filled out by women who are attorneys themselves. Their comments:

"I don't trust it (mediation). They don't know

all the legal angles, future possibilities....."

"I think an attorney is better equipped."

"A lawyer was required for my purposes."

In five cases, a lawyer was, in essence, part of the family. Three women reported that their spouses were attorneys themselves. One man noted that his wife's father was a lawyer, and one that his wife's new boyfriend was.

In ten cases, the spouse reportedly insisted on having his or her own attorney. (In one unusual case, however, the wife was reported to have hired a "friendly" lawyer, making mediation unnecessary in the husband's opinion. At least one woman reported that her husband appeared to like the repeated delays caused by the legal system.

### Reason: Issues Too Complex -- Or Too Simple

The third most frequently cited reason given as an answer to the question "Why you and your spouse did not use mediation" was the complexity of the issues involved in the divorce. Fourteen subjects (12.3 percent) mentioned this aspect of the divorce. Men were more likely to cite this reason. Nine of the 14 were male; five were female. For both sexes, financial and legal issues were mentioned most often, followed by the questions of custody and child care. Residency and inequitable property demands also were cited.

Ten subjects (8.8 percent) answered question 20 by stating that mediation was unnecessary because the divorce was so easy, so amicable or involved such simple issues. This response was evenly divided between men and women. Terms were worked out between the two, either with no outside assistance at all or using friends as mediators of sorts.

## Mediation Seen as Reconciliation

Although a pamphlet on divorce mediation was enclosed in the questionnaire mailing, at least eight subjects (7 percent) appeared to have misconceptions about mediation and its purpose.

It seems that some saw mediation as an attempt at reconciliation. Seven of the eight subjects who did so were men.

> "I wanted out of the relationship -- positively."
> -- Engineer
> Male, no age given

> "We are both happier alone."
> -- Entrepreneur
> Male, age 40

> "Nothing to mediate. She wanted her freedom and independence."
> -- Supervisor
> Male, age 43

> "Growing apart. Different interests. Married young, for all the wrong reasons. No mature approach as to who we were, what we wanted out of life, goals, etc."
> -- Sales rep
> Male, age 48

One woman answered:

> "There was no solution to the problems -- We both wanted completely different things out of life and very different values. So much for whirlwind romance."
> -- Elementary school teacher
> Female, age 35

In addition to these more common responses, several other categories of response turned up for this question. Two subjects mentioned mistrust (of both the spouse and the mediator), one mentioned the need for an investigation, one answered "business reasons" and one man answered question 20 with a single word, "mean."

The survey's final question asked subjects whether they would recommend mediation to friends considering divorce. Of the 366 who responded to question 21, 253 (69.1 percent) checked "yes." An additional 58 (15.8 percent) answered that it would depend on the situation. This adds up to an impressive 84.9 percent of subjects who would, at least under some circumstances, recommend the mediation process to people they know.

Men tended to be slightly more positive than women. Of the 165 men who answered this question, 119 (72.1 percent) said yes and 23 (13.9 percent) said that it depended on the situation. Of the 201 women who responded, 134 (66.7 percent) said yes and 35 (17.4 percent) said that it depended.

The percentages answering no and not sure were closer. Of males, 10.3 percent answered no and 3.6 percent answered not sure. Of females, 11.9 percent answered no and 4 percent answered not sure.

A number of subjects took the opportunity of question 21 and the blank space beneath it to write comments, some bordering on short essays, on the topics of divorce and mediation.

> "I would advise it, depending on  the circum-
> stances of the couple...my husband and I did
> not want to get involved with the courts,
> because we had seen (sic) many couples end up
> at war with one another."
>           -- Teacher
>           Female, age 33

"It depends on the attitudes of the two people

and the ability to find a competent mediator.
The spouse that is willing to compromise gets
screwed in mediation!"
                    -- Computer systems specialist
                    Male, age 35


"If the situation warrants one.  Perhaps you
market marriage contracts."
                    -- Advertising copywriter
                    Female, no age given


"Yes (or else to shoot his wife and get a South
Philly lawyer, rather than see an attorney)."
                    -- Manager
                    Male, age 41


"I would advise any woman/man to go for immediate
divorce and not waste any time.  Find a lawyer
and end it while the one who's left is feeling
guilty and desperate...."
                    -- Teacher
                    Female, age 43


"We attempted mediation.  Unfortunately the
mediator was a family counselor who was grossly
ignorant re(garding) divorce finances, legalities and who

had not understood the difference between divorce
mediation and family counselling."
                    -- Physicist
                    Male, age 40


"My divorce became a personal fight between the
two lawyers -- his & mine -- it became their
'win or loss.'"
                    -- Office manager
                    Female, age 45

"It seems people who would use/benefit/be agree-
able to a mediator do not need divorces.  It's
the irrational, unreasonable people who would
benefit, but they're the ones who would never
use a mediator."

-- Executive
Male, age 38

# REFERENCES

Abel, J., B. Fontes, B. Greenberg, and C. Atkin. *The Impact of Television on Children's Occupational Role Learning.* East Lansing: Michigan State University, 1981.

Blades, J. "Mediation: An Old Art Revisited." Quoted in J.A. Lemmon,ed., "Reaching Effective Agreements," *Mediation Quarterly 3* (March 1984).

Burnkrant, R.E. and A. Cousineau. "Informational and Normative Social Influence in Buyer Behavior." *Journal of Consumer Research,* (December 1975). Cited in Runyon and Stewart, *Consumer Behavior and the Practice of Marketing.* Columbus, Ohio: Merrill Publishing, 1987.

Curtis, S. and D. Akins. "Effective Marketing: How Firms Can Improve Their Image." *Trial Magazine,* (December 1984).

Dewey, J. *How We Think.* Boston, MA: D.C. Heath, 1910.

French, J.R.P. and B. Raven. *The Bases of Social Power.* Quoted in Carwright, D., ed, *Studies in Social Power* (Ann Arbor, MI: The University of Michigan's Institute for Social Research, 1959)

Gardner, M. P. "Mood States and Consumer Behavior: A Critical Review." *Journal of Consumer Research 12* (December 1985).

Gates, A. *90 Most Promising Careers for the 80s.* New York: Monarch Press, 1982.

Ingrasci, H.J. "How to Reach Buyers in Their Psychological Comfort Zones." *Industrial Marketing* (July 1981).

Jeffries-Fox, S. and Signorielli. 1982. Television and Children's Conceptions of Occupations. Paper presented at the Airlid House Telecommunications Conference, Warrenton, VA.

Jones, L.Y. "The Baby-Boomer Consumer." *American Demographics*, (February 1981). Reprinted in Hoel, R.F., ed., *The Dynamics of Marketing: Current Happenings in the Marketplace*. New York: Harper &Row, 1982.

Katz, D. "The Functional Approach to the Study of Attitudes." *Public Opinion Quarterly 24* (1960).

Katz, E. and P.F. Lazarsfeld. *Personal Influence*. New York: MacMillan Publishing, 1955. Cited in Runyon and Stewart, *Consumer Behavior and the Practice of Marketing*. Columbus, Ohio: Merrill Publishing, 1987.

Kelly, J. "Mediated and Adversarial Divorce: Respondents' Perceptions of Their Processes and Outcomes." Quoted in J. B. Kelly, ed., *Mediation Quarterly 24* (1989).

Lipset, S. "The Value Patterns of Democracy: A Case Study in Comparative Values." *American Sociological Review 28* (August 1963).

Maslow, A. H. *Motivation and Personality*. New York: Harper and Row, 1970.

Murray, H.A., ed., *Explanations in Personality*. Oxford University Press, 1938.

National Institute for Mental Health (NIMH). *Television and Behavior: Ten Years of Scientific Progress and Implications for the Eighties*. Vol.1, 1982.

Practicing Law Institute. "Through a Glass Hopefully." *Marketing for Today's Law Firm*, 1986. Reprinted in Burke, E.J. *Marketing for Law Firms*. New York: Law Journal Seminars-Press, 1987.

Riesman, D., N. Glazer, and Denney, R. *The Lonely Crowd*. New Haven, Connecticut: Yale University Press, 1950. Quoted in Runyon and Stewart, *Consumer Behavior and the Practice of Marketing*. Columbus, Ohio: Merrill Publishing, 1987.

Runyon, K.E. and D.W. Stewart. *Consumer Behavior and the Practice of Marketing*. Columbus, Ohio: Merrill Publishing Co., 1987.

Shartsis, A.J. "Is Marketing for Everyone?" *ABA Journal - The Lawyer's Magazine*. January 1986. Reprinted in Burke, E.J. *Marketing for Law Firms*. New York: Law Journal Seminars-Press, 1987.

Shimp, T. A. and A. Kavas "The Theory of Reasoned Action Applied to Coupon Usage." *Journal of Consumer Research 2*, (December 1984).

Slaby, R.G. and G.R. Quarforth. "Effects of Television on the Developing Child." Quoted in B. W. Camp, ed., "Advances in Behavioral Pediatrics 1," 1980.

Witt, R.E. and G.D. Bruce. "Group Influence and Brand Choice Congruence," *Journal of Marketing Research 9*, 1972. Cited in Runyon and Stewart, *Consumer Behavior and the Practice of Marketing*. Columbus, Ohio: Merrill Publishing, 1987.

## About the Author

**Joyce Hauser** (Ph.D.) is presently Assistant Professor at New York University in The School of Education. She was president and chief operating officer of three major corporations in the field of communications -- advertising, public relations, and marketing. The client roster included American Dental Association, League of Voluntary Hospitals, American Psychiatric Association and many illustrious private and publicly held corporations.

Since 1985, Dr. Hauser has served as a mediator and arbitrator for the Victim Services Agency, the Institute for Mediation and Conflict Resolution, and also practiced as a private family and divorce mediator. Appointed to the American Arbitration Association panel of arbitrators, a member of the Academy of Family Mediators, and vice-president for the New York State Speech Communication Association, she has lectured and written extensively on Mediation and Family Communications. Dr. Hauser currently teaches Communications courses, including Mediation, Group Dynamics, advanced issues in Non-Verbal Communication, and Public Relations.

For thirteen years, she was a broadcaster and producer for NBC-Radio hosting her own series "Conversations with Joyce Hauser," an interview-discussion format; her guests included Golda Meier, Margaret Mead, Richard Nixon, Margaret Thatcher and Dali Lama and many other luminaries in the arts, politics and science. She also hosted "What's On Your Mind," a call-in program, which reviewed the topical and often the highly personal. She was also a host for Talk-Net and served as moderator on WNEW-TV and WOR-TV.

Named one of the Top Twenty Women in Public Relations in the United States and awarded the title of "Top Fifteen American Women" by the National Cancer Society, she is included in Marquis' "Who's Who in the World, In The East, In Industry and Finance, In Advertising, and American Women."